BREAKING BARRIERS

BREAKING BARRIERS

Working and Loving While Blind

A Memoir

PETER ALTSCHUL, MS

iUniverse, Inc.
Bloomington

Breaking Barriers
Working and Loving While Blind

Names have been changed, not for reasons of privacy but for cases in which the author knew more than one person with the same first name.

iUniverse books may be ordered through booksellers or by contacting:

iUniverse
1663 Liberty Drive
Bloomington, IN 47403
www.iuniverse.com
1-800-Authors (1-800-288-4677)

ISBN: 978-1-4697-3111-7 (sc)
ISBN: 978-1-4697-3113-1 (hc)
ISBN: 978-1-4697-3112-4 (e)

Printed in the United States of America

iUniverse rev. date: 05/15/2012

To my wife, Lisa,
who is teaching me how to love.

PREFACE

This book sprang from a journal I wrote while learning to work with my fifth guide dog, a black Labrador retriever named Jules. Every morning for nearly a month, I would e-mail my daily adventures to family, friends, and business associates, and the feedback was overwhelmingly positive. Several encouraged me to write a book. But I dislike writing, so I filed away these suggestions.

Eighteen months later, I moved to Columbia, Missouri, to be with the woman I love. "You should write a book," she told me after I had read her the Jules journal. Ultimately, I overcame my reluctance after she encouraged me to take an advanced nonfiction writing course at the University of Missouri. During the next five years, the journal gradually morphed into this book.

My main aim is to tell a good story through a unique prism: totally blind person blazes unique professional trail with the assistance and companionship of five guide dogs, and then unexpectedly falls in love and gets married at the age of fifty. Along the way, I wanted to describe how a specially trained dog and man meet and meld into a smooth working team and how dogs can subtly affect what's happening around them. I wanted to think about what distinguishes effective from ineffective organizations. I wanted to reflect on how I addressed the challenges I faced with or without support from the people and social structures around me. I wanted to address how ceremonies can either energize or demoralize those who participate in them. And perhaps most importantly, I wanted to convey that people with visual impairments are neither godlike nor pathetic pawns, and that the dogs that assist us are terrific—but they are dogs, not beings with superhuman abilities to read minds and leap tall buildings. Those who either put us on a pedestal or drown us with pity make it more difficult for us to work and to love.

ACKNOWLEDGMENTS

This book would have never been written without encouraging words and constructive feedback from family and friends, most of whom are written about in the following pages. But special thanks go to the folks at iUniverse who have patiently guided me through the publishing process, especially Don Seitz, Rebekka Potter, Sarah Disbrow, Andrea Long, and the folks on the design team. Thanks, Leah Johnson of Johnson Photography, for working with this reluctant picture-poser to create the cover photos. Thanks to the staff at Guiding Eyes for the Blind, especially Graham Buck and Becky Barnes, not just for their great work but for providing me with background information concerning the training of guide dogs. Thanks to my mom and sister for helping me to grow up and to reconnect with some of my childhood memories. Betina Drew, a former University of Missouri professor, was enormously helpful in encouraging me to use shorter words and to abstain from writing in bureaucratese. And a very special thank-you to my wife Lisa who held both my physical and emotional hands throughout this process.

TABLE OF CONTENTS

Prologue: Pet Dogs and Working Dogs 1

Part I: Dog Days

Chapter One: Preparing for the New Dog. 15

Chapter Two: The New Dog 28

Chapter Three: Play Day 39

Chapter Four: Back to Work 50

Chapter Five: Preparing to Leave. 59

Part II: Home Training

Chapter Six: Home Alone with Jules 77

Chapter Seven: Patterning. 85

Chapter Eight: Onstage. 94

Chapter Nine: Making Connections 107

Part III: Saying Good-byes

Chapter Ten: A Dunbar Factor 125

Chapter Eleven: The Trip to Trenton 138

Chapter Twelve: The Eulogy 149

Part IV: Saying Hello

Chapter Thirteen: What Happens in Vegas 163

Chapter Fourteen: The Blessings 176

Chapter Fifteen: Control. 187

Chapter Sixteen: Loosening Ties 196

Chapter Seventeen: Three Ceremonies 205

Epilogue: Family Man. 223

PROLOGUE:
PET DOGS AND WORKING DOGS

For some unknown reason, I was born totally blind. I grew up in Pleasantville, New York, a working-class town an hour north of New York City. My mom juggled parenting, teaching, cooking, cleaning, gardening, building, and other tasks related to the care of a large, noisy two-story house. My dad taught chemistry at Sarah Lawrence College, a small, well-respected liberal arts school about forty-five minutes from our house. My sister, Jenny, who has normal eyesight, was born a year later.

Mom wanted me to go to a school with sighted peers instead of a boarding school for blind students because she believed I would get a better education while living at home. "Your blind son cannot come here," the headmaster of a small private school thirty minutes from our house told her when I was ready to enter kindergarten. "He should be attending a school for blind children." But I did attend that school through eighth grade, and that is where I learned to read, write, and count. I played fullback during gym class soccer games where I could get in the way of unsuspecting forwards by listening to the progress of foot meeting ball. I also began learning how to play the piano and bang on the drums.

Because I was the only blind student at the school, Mom knew that she would have to spend more time, energy, creativity, patience, and smarts than other parents so that I could take part in school activities on an almost

1

equal footing. But she relished the challenge. She learned braille and taught me how to read by the time I was five. She worked with teachers who were uncomfortable having a blind kid in their class. She taught me the skills I would need to live independently. She ordered textbooks in braille or on tape from agencies serving blind people and spent many afternoons and evenings transcribing materials into braille while the rest of the family relaxed or slept. She created maps, graphs, and other "tactile drawings" using nails, foam rubber, sandpaper, and other common materials that I could explore by touch. And when materials weren't available, she read them to me.

When I was in the eighth grade, Mom decided that I needed a change. While my grades were good, I was running with the wrong crowd and causing too much trouble. She persuaded the leaders of the local public high school to accept me the following year. Her marketing pitch to me was tempting: that I could take advantage of the broader array of courses and activities there; that I would be able to walk to and from school once I learned how to use a long white cane; and that she wouldn't talk to any of my teachers or even set foot in the school. "I'm out of it," she had said. "It's up to you whether you succeed or fail."

Once again, I was the only blind student, and I spent much of my first year adjusting to the larger building, the noisier halls full of strangers, and the larger classes. Over time, I connected with the musicians and athletes as I played drums in the band and organ in local churches, joined the wrestling team, and sang in several choirs.

Mom kept her promise of not interfering with my school life until the final semester of my senior year. I was eating lunch with friends when a piece of paper was thrust into my hand.

"I can't believe it," she said, her voice quivering with excitement.

Startled, I began reading what turned out to be my acceptance letter from Princeton University, which she had brailled immediately after receiving the official letter in print.

"Isn't that wonderful?" she nearly shouted.

I grunted, fearing the reaction of those around me. I had tried to sell myself as a regular guy with smarts instead of an intellectual egghead.

"Nancy! What are you doing here?" the music director asked Mom. She shared the news, and soon I was surrounded by a group of admirers showering me with congratulations and advice.

A couple of weeks later, Mom met me at the door of our house to tell me that some sort of counselor would be visiting the next day. I grunted over my shoulder as I headed upstairs to my room, where I stood my cane in a corner. "I know we don't like these people," she called after me, "but we need to be nice to her because she might help with the tuition."

The following afternoon, a woman reeking of perfume told us in a quiet, syrupy voice that she was a vocational rehabilitation counselor at the New York State Commission for the Blind and Visually Handicapped. She explained that they taught blind people to read and write braille, travel with a cane, use a typewriter, and other skills I had already mastered, as well as providing assistance in finding a job. When we explained that I had been accepted at Princeton, she questioned if I was ready for college and told us that they couldn't provide any financial aid unless I went to a school in New York State. When we informed her that we had already committed to Princeton, she told us that they might be able to give us money if I attended a month-long program aimed at preparing blind people for college. "Sorry," Mom said, "but Peter will be taking part in a summer-long program for gifted musicians."

Despite our unwillingness to cooperate, the Commission for the Blind did provide some financial aid that, when combined with a scholarship from Sarah Lawrence College and financial support from my grandmother, made it possible for me to afford the tuition. At Princeton, I continued sparring with my VR counselor. Every semester, she would threaten to withhold funding because, while my grades were solid, the commission required a grade point average that Princeton didn't calculate as part of their transcripts. Twice a year, I dashed off a letter, giving her just enough information to keep her out of my life. Every year, I wasted a summer afternoon taking part in a meeting of blind college students at her office. During one of these meetings, she asked me to share a piece of advice with my fellow students.

"Don't do all your homework," I suggested.

"What?" she squawked.

I explained that while I did most of my homework most of the time, I also played percussion in the orchestra, marching band, and jazz ensemble, and that I had joined one of the more prestigious "eating clubs" (similar to fraternities on other campuses), where I hung out with the boys and partied a bit too much. "College is more than coursework," I declared, enjoying my counselor's discomfort, "and most students learn which assignments to ignore so that they can make friends and engage in other activities—"

"You mean set goals!" she snapped.

~

DOGS WERE A CENTRAL PART of our family. Suzie, a black Labrador retriever, was nine months old when I was born, and Molly, another black Lab, arrived when I was eight. They crashed through the underbrush as Jenny and I walked in the woods with Mom and Dad near our Pleasantville home and swam in the ocean and the lakes on Cape Cod, Massachusetts, where my parents had bought a small, run-down cottage when I was three years old. We threw things for the dogs to retrieve and played tug-of-war using an old pair of rolled-up jeans with a knot at each end. And we shared our deepest secrets with them as we ruffled their thick coats and scratched behind their soft ears.

When I was nine years old, I became interested in guide dogs after meeting a couple of blind adults who used them. During my sophomore year of high school, I began receiving newsletters in braille from Guiding Eyes for the Blind, a small nonprofit organization thirty minutes north of Pleasantville. At that time, Guiding Eyes was the second organization that trained German shepherds, Labrador retrievers, and other breeds to lead a blind person safely from place to place, matched each dog with a person, and supported each team as they learned to work together. These newsletters shared entertaining examples of the adventures of these person-dog partnerships, and by the time I graduated from high school, I was hooked on the idea of working with a Guiding Eyes dog.

But I didn't apply until I graduated from college because living around dogs made me realize that the long rehearsals and road trips connected with my music-making, when combined with my coursework and beer-drinking binges, wouldn't be a good environment for a dog. I continued using a cane to get to where I needed to go, and I found myself being hyper alert so I could react to the information it transmitted as it bounced off and around obstacles several feet in front of me. A week before I graduated, several of my eating-club friends gave me a T-shirt with the words "Move, or I'll stick my cane up your ass" written in print letters large enough for me to feel. As I proudly put on the shirt and laughed along with others in the room, I remembered someone telling me that using a cane is a contact sport. While the shirt honored my tendency to use the cane to clear human obstacles in my path, I thought that a dog might be a faster, more relaxing, and less obnoxious way to get around, in addition to providing companionship and entertainment.

Upon graduating in 1979, I spent nearly a month at Guiding Eyes learning to work with Heidi, a Weimaraner with a large repertoire of barks, howls, and grunts. During the next eight years, she assisted me through the streets of Boston and the halls of New England Conservatory, where I obtained a master's degree in music composition. She assisted me through the streets of New York City as I tried to break into the music business and landed my first job doing customer service work for a large, federal government agency.

In 1987, Heidi needed to retire because of the arthritis in her back legs. We returned to Guiding Eyes, where a childless couple from Connecticut welcomed her into their home a day before I was matched with Nan, a chocolate Labrador who licked anyone she could reach. She was with me as I changed jobs to work at a call center for a large, stodgy bank on Wall Street where I was the only blind person in the office. When the bank outsourced my job to a call center in Jacksonville, Florida, she was at my side at Columbia University's School of Social Work, where I learned about assisting individuals, groups, and organizations in becoming more effective. Six months after receiving my master's degree in social work, I landed a job managing a nationwide project aimed at improving employment opportunities for college students with disabilities at a nonprofit organization where I was the only blind employee.

In 1994, Nan and I returned to Guiding Eyes. After their veterinarian removed a lump from her side, she moved in with an interior decorator who lived in Manhattan. Meanwhile, I was matched with Dunbar, a black Lab who was a skilled food thief. He was with me as I assisted school districts throughout New York State in redesigning the way technology was made available to students with disabilities and conducted workshops to encourage New York City taxi drivers to treat their passengers more humanely. In 1998, we moved to Washington, DC, where I had landed a job at a small nongovernment organization (NGO) forming and working with groups of pro-life and pro-choice activists. I was the first blind person they had ever hired.

In 1999, Gifford, a black Lab with a constantly wagging tail, replaced Dunbar, whose pace had slowed during the past six months. As he lived out his retirement years with Linda and Pat Walters, two health-care professionals who enjoy pampering retired guide dogs, Gifford guided me through the streets of Washington, DC, and New York City as I helped a large NGO to develop programs to improve the way it hired and retained people with disabilities. I served as a consultant at a large management consulting firm where I was the first blind person they had ever hired. I assisted a large London-based corporation in developing its diversity initiative where again I was told that I was the first blind person they had hired. During vacations, we visited my mom and her laid-back golden retrievers on Cape Cod, and my dad; Pat, my stepmother; and Happy, their bossy toy poodle, in central New Jersey.

In June 2004, I alerted Guiding Eyes that Gifford would soon be ready to retire, as his pace was slowing and his enthusiasm was waning. An instructor visited me to ask what I wanted in a new dog and to observe me working with Gifford, and in January 2005, an admissions representative told me that a dog would be ready in March.

Transitioning between dogs prompted sadness and anticipation: sadness in retiring a cheerful, faithful friend who was still propelling me to large office buildings, restaurants, airports, and train stations, and anticipation concerning what new creature awaited me. As March approached, I cuddled with Gifford, telling him how wonderful he was and how hard he would be to replace as he wagged his tail, rolled on his back, or snored lustily. I regaled friends with stories of our adventures together: how a tendon in his right front leg had been sliced in a taxi, requiring emergency surgery and a month's convalescence before we could work together again; how a car had grazed my right arm as we were hurrying to a meeting; and how after a blizzard had dropped two feet of snow, we had to walk for half a mile every day for a month on the shoulder of an eight-lane highway in order to get to my job because town officials refused to shovel the sidewalks. And then there were the amusingly irritating encounters with strangers.

"What a handsome dog!" a pedestrian would say as Gifford wagged his tail. "What's his name?"

"Gifford."

"Like the cartoon character!" they would chirp. "Hi, Clifford. Can I pet him?"

"I'm sorry, but you can't pet *Gifford* because he's working when his harness is on."

"I understand," the pedestrian would sigh while turning away. "Good-bye, Clifford!"

As March drew closer, I pared back my professional life so I could concentrate on learning to work with a new dog. I made arrangements for Gifford to live with Linda and Pat Walters. I spent my last day before flying to Guiding Eyes working him to a fast-food restaurant in a late winter storm. I packed clothes, toiletries, a radio, headphones, and braille magazines. I also packed my Braille Lite, a two-pound piece of technology that is a cross between a Palm Pilot and a laptop computer that I used to read and write articles, books, and reports. I assured family and friends that I would let them know about my new dog as soon as I could.

While Gifford snored from the couch, I reflected that while I was an experienced guide dog user, I still had much to learn. I had heard that Guiding Eyes had added some new wrinkles to their training. And I would have to adapt to my new dog's unique quirks.

The Walters arrived at 6:30 the next morning to drive Gifford and me to Reagan National Airport. He whimpered softly as I put my arms around him.

"He knows," Linda said in wonder.

"Good-bye, Gifford," I cooed. "I'll miss you and will never forget you." I turned to Linda. "I know you will take good care of him," I said with a lump in my throat as we walked to the ticket counter.

"Don't worry; looking after him is a privilege." We hugged as an airline employee arrived to assist me to the gate.

Peter and Heidi; taken in the Peter Campbell Lounge
at Guiding Eyes for the Blind; August, 1979

Peter and Nan; taken in the Peter Campbell Lounge at
Guiding Eyes for the Blind; August, 1987

Peter and Dunbar; taken in the Peter Campbell Lounge
at Guiding Eyes for the Blind; August, 1994

Peter and Gifford; taken in my DC apartment; November, 1999

PART I:

DOG DAYS

CHAPTER ONE:
PREPARING FOR THE NEW DOG

~

MARCH 1–2, 2005

At LaGuardia Airport, I held onto the left elbow of an airport employee with my suitcase in my right hand and my backpack on my back. As he guided me toward the security area, an unfamiliar voice identified herself as Jolene from Guiding Eyes. "Hi!" I called back. As we drew even with her, I thanked the airport employee for his help and transferred my grip to Jolene's elbow without breaking stride. She led me out of the bustling, warm dryness of the airport to the cold, damp pavement of the sidewalk. Cars and buses sloshed past us as we approached the van in which two students and I would be driven to the school. I handed her my suitcase, which she stowed in the back as I climbed in. She introduced me to a woman in the van named Pam, rolled the door shut, and went back into the terminal.

Pam told me that she was an instructor's assistant working in the kennel taking care of dogs-in-training. She had recently been assigned to assist the instructors who would be teaching us how to work with our new dogs. Over time, she would develop the needed skills to work with both dogs and people with visual impairments.

We soon discovered that we knew people in common because we both had worked for small NGOs that tried to tackle the world's biggest conflicts. I asked what had prompted the career change.

"I've always loved dogs, and I got tired of the frantic pace," she said as Jolene assisted the second student into the van.

After the doors rolled shut, Pam asked me about my work. I told her about a reverse mentoring program I was running for the American branch of a large London-based corporation as part of its diversity initiative. I explained that this program "flipped" the usual mentoring relationship; instead of a more senior person mentoring a more junior person, the more junior person took on the mentoring role.

"Fascinating. How did you get the idea?"

I explained that I had been looking for a low-cost way to assist the organization's leadership team in understanding the barriers that made it more difficult for people other than white men to get ahead, and how I had overheard someone at a conference describing a bank's effort to start a program where people from diverse backgrounds mentored senior managers about diversity and culture change. "The simplicity and uniqueness of the idea got my attention," I told her.

"How's it going?" she asked as I heard Jolene approach the van with the third student.

"Very well." The third student boarded, and the door rolled shut. "I'm supposed to write a report summarizing its successes while I'm at the school."

"Welcome to Guiding Eyes," Jolene called. She started the van. "We should be there in about an hour."

As the van eased into traffic, Pam asked if I would be writing the report using one of the computers that the school has available for its students. "You know that we installed both of those software programs with the weird names that convert what's on the screen into speech?"

I laughed. "You mean JAWS and Window-eyes?"

"Yes. I have a lot to learn."

I told Pam that while I used JAWS (Job Access with Speech) to listen to the text on the screen, I would write my report using my Braille Lite. I took it out of my backpack and showed her how text is input using the six braille keys instead of the QWRTY keyboard. I explained that material is input as ASCII text and can be converted to a Microsoft Word or WordPerfect file on any personal computer. I demonstrated how I could read text by running my fingers along the braille display at the front of the machine or listen to it using its robotic-sounding "voice."

After a period of sparse chitchat, I eased into a conversation with a middle-aged woman from North Carolina who had recently ended her relationship with an abusive husband. She described how many of her friends had discouraged her from leaving. "He's such a nice man," they had said, "and how will you be able to live without him? You're blind."

"I'm glad you left him," I told her.

She said that she was fine living alone but that she was having trouble with her VR counselor.

I cringed. "What's the problem?"

"She won't return my calls. She's very condescending and won't help me get the training I need to get a job."

"Sounds familiar." I sighed and began describing the strategy I used when my VR counselor wouldn't return my calls.

"I had just received my master's in music," I explained, "and I was sharing a small studio apartment in Manhattan with my first guide dog, a Weimaraner named Heidi. I was trying to break into the music business."

"Doing what?" someone asked.

"I wanted to write music jingles for commercials," I said. "I also enjoyed writing and producing pop tunes."

"Were you successful?"

"Not really. Heidi and I spent two years knocking on doors, and while I did get one tune published and made some money recording tracks for other songwriters, I concluded that I wasn't cut out for the business. So I took the first job I could get: doing customer service work for a large federal government agency.

"Anyway," I continued, "twice a year I would receive a letter in print from my counselor threatening to close my case if I didn't contact her immediately. First I had to find someone sighted to read the letter. Then I would call and ask to speak with my counselor, and the receptionist always told me that she wasn't available. I would politely ask that my counselor call me back.

"Of course she would never return my call," I said as the passengers snickered, "and I would call back the receptionist two or three days later and threaten to sue or to call the media or to organize a demonstration or anything else I could think of short of physical violence, and my counselor always called me back within an hour."

"That's rude!" Jolene's voice cut through our laughter.

"That's what my counselor said. She also accused me of threatening the receptionist."

"What did you say?" asked another passenger, who sounded like an elderly African American gentleman.

"The truth—that the only way she would return my calls was if I threatened to take action."

"I don't think I could get away with that."

"Probably not," I muttered. I feared voicing my belief that I had probably gotten away with my threats in part because I was white and a recent graduate from two elite universities. If he'd tried something like that, his VR counselor might have called the cops.

"I still say you were rude!" Jolene repeated.

"Of course I was rude. And the sad thing is that many other clients of the VR system use similar tactics to get results from their counselors. Then they try the same approach at work and wonder why they don't get along with their bosses."

"We're here," Jolene announced several minutes later as she turned the van into the driveway. As we got out, she carried our luggage inside while assisting us into the lobby. During the next ten minutes, instructors showed each of us how to walk to our rooms and oriented us to the location of the beds, Internet connections, desks, chairs, radios/CD players, bathrooms, and the door leading to the area where our new dogs would go to the bathroom. They used a combination of audible and tactile techniques. "Peter," one of the instructors said, "your room is the third on the right." He tapped several times on the door frame and put my right hand on the room number in braille and large print about five feet off the ground near each door handle. Instructors were also available to assist us in learning how to get to the dining room and other locations throughout the building. This was important because guide dogs are trained to assist their handlers in walking safely from one place to another. They are not responsible for deciding on which route to take. We must know how to get to where we want to go and then communicate it to our dogs using verbal commands and hand gestures.

After lunch, unpacking, and some quiet time, I attended our first formal meeting in the Peter Campbell Lounge where I had spent many hours over the years listening to lectures, talking with my fellow students, and playing the piano. Eileen and Erik, the two instructors, opened the meeting by introducing themselves and then encouraged us to become acquainted. The twelve of us lived throughout the United States and Canada. Our ages ranged from the early twenties to the late seventies. The level of visual acuity ranged from total blindness to the ability to read materials in large print and to travel during daylight hours without guide dog or cane. Our community also included Pam, the instructor's assistant, and Melinda, the class supervisor.

Erik and Eileen next reviewed the guidelines that would govern the life of our small community.

"Talk to each other so people know where you are," Eileen suggested, "especially when you get your dogs in a couple of days."

"And please be extra careful when you are carrying hot coffee," Erik added, "because we don't want any dog or person burned. If you spill something, either clean it up or let us know; the floors can get very slippery."

"Try to help each other out," Eileen continued. "If someone says they are looking for a chair and there is one next to you, direct them to it."

As the instructors encouraged us not to drink too much alcohol; to show up on time for meals, meetings, and trips; not to smoke in the building; to treat each other respectfully; and to keep our dogs out of the way so they would not be stepped on, I thought about my first stay at Guiding Eyes twenty-six years earlier. It was the first time I had been around adults who were blind. I was a cocky recent college graduate who had played percussion in the marching band, orchestra, and jazz ensemble. I had recently visited Washington, DC, courtesy of Recording for the Blind (now Learning Ally) who had selected two other blind college seniors and me for a national award honoring academic excellence. While there, I had visited then-Senator Bill Bradley, a Princeton alumnus; attended a banquet at the National Science Foundation to honor us student scholars; and shaken the hand of then-Vice President Walter Mondale. I had just learned that the Princeton Chapel Choir would be performing a mass that I had written during my senior year.

I also believed that rules were for wimps, having spent most of my life finding ways to work around them. I started fighting my own battles one month into my high school experience.

"What do you mean you won't allow me to lift weights?" I had shouted at the well-respected football coach. This outburst had resulted in horrified gasps from bystanders and the chance to lift weights.

During my freshman year at Princeton, the conductor of the wind ensemble refused to allow me into the group because I couldn't follow his hand signals. I thought I would lose this battle despite my vehement objections; after all, I had been in my high school's concert band for three years and successfully auditioned for the All-County Band during my senior year. But I went to a wind ensemble concert several months later and noticed that the sighted percussionists the conductor had imported from another college failed to follow his lead.

"Did you notice how those percussionists—"

"We know," several student band officers chimed in exasperated unison.

A year later, the conductor was gone, and his replacement welcomed me into the group.

So I had ignored one of the Guiding Eyes rules by not announcing my presence as I walked through the building; after all, I didn't tell sighted people where I was, so why tell blind people? My fellow students would bump into me and then want to know why I hadn't let them know where I was so they could get out of my way. I would offer a half-hearted "sorry" and move on. When enough people complained about my rudeness, I changed my approach.

"I'm here! Coming through!" I would trumpet as I approached a doorway.

"You make my ears hurt," students complained.

I knew I was announcing my presence in a loud voice to rebel against the rules. That was just how I was at the time. But the passage of years can mellow a man, and as I listened to the instructors give us our marching orders, I relaxed. I knew the rules, and they made sense.

"And one more thing," Eileen said, "when you get your dogs, please focus on looking after your own dog."

"And don't judge others because they don't take care of their dog the same way that you do," Erik added.

"We know that this is a stressful experience, and we want to make your stay as pleasant as possible," Eileen said, "so please don't hesitate to call us if you need help. Any questions? No? Then it's time for dinner."

As the dinner clatter picked up, I thought about how each of us had left family, friends, and familiar surroundings to live at Guiding Eyes with eleven other students with visual impairments from different backgrounds. While a few students stay for twelve days, others stay for eighteen days or even for nearly a month. The length of stay depends upon the experience of the student and the success of the match between student and dog. "How many other people would take this leap of faith?" I asked myself as I began cutting up my chicken breast.

After dinner, we attended our first lecture in which Erik talked about the "Slip Collar," a piece of chain with a metal ring at each end; the leather leash; and the harness, which consists of the frame into which the dog's body fits and a rigid handle that each of us holds onto and through which each of us learns to gauge our dog's moves through subtle vibrations.

I drank a beer with two Vietnam vets after the lecture in the Coffee Room, an uncarpeted space containing several round tables and plastic chairs, along with a coffee machine, water cooler, microwave oven, refrigerator, and bowls filled with fruit and other snacks. I felt out of place as they reminisced about their wartime experiences and irritated as they heaped praise on President George W. Bush for sending troops to Iraq "to kill all those fucking Arab terrorists." Not wishing to get into a political argument, I said a curt "good night" and trudged to my room feeling alone and a little annoyed. I tuned the radio to WCBS News Radio 88, a station that had provided useful information and background noise for more than twenty-five years as I completed homework assignments and household chores. With the radio playing softly, I crawled into bed and quickly fell asleep.

"Good morning; it's 6:30 a.m.," Erik's voice intoned through the PA system. "Breakfast will be at seven."

As I got ready, I wished that the day could be skipped so that I could meet my new dog. While the reasons for the delay made sense, I wasn't looking forward to taking part in activities I had gone through several times already.

"Good morning, beautiful people!" Jose called in a lilting Spanish accent as we started eating our breakfasts. He had greeted classes with this phrase for the past thirty years, first as chief chef and later as the director of housekeeping. During my first stay at Guiding Eyes, he had encouraged me to treat my fellow students more kindly and had found the right thing to say when I became irritated with those rules made for wimps.

"Good morning, Jose," we responded with varied degrees of alertness.

As Jose explained how things would work in the dining room, it occurred to me how much more relaxed and engaged I had suddenly become. It's remarkable what a cheerful word from an influential person in a well-respected organization can do.

I was neither relaxed nor engaged during my first week at my first job where my fellow employees and I had been confined to a large airless room. We had completed a mind-numbing amount of paperwork. We had listened to endless presentations about the glories of the organization from faceless bureaucrats who we never heard from again. We spent way too much time sitting around doing nothing. During the next six weeks, we received training from instructors who we would never talk to again. We would soon find out that the information we learned was only slightly helpful as we spent most of our time listening to customer questions, filling out the proper form, and explaining that we would forward the information to our research unit who would get back to them within three to six weeks.

I was slightly more engaged during the early stages of my second job. At the stodgy bank on Wall Street, I joined a small group of fellow employees in a stuffy carpeted room where we filled out forms and listened to faceless bureaucrats rhapsodize about the bank's glorious history. During the next month, our supervisors taught us the information we would need to address the concerns of the customers we would be speaking with over the phone. This training was more useful because we had access to much of the information we would need to help those who called us.

There weren't many cheerful words from supervisors at either job, I thought as we all groaned at one of Jose's corny jokes. And there were other reasons I felt more connected to Guiding Eyes. I had forged sound working relationships with four Guiding Eyes dogs. I was far more committed to becoming a great partner for this new dog than answering phone calls from strangers for thirty-five hours a week. And as we milled about waiting for Eric and Eileen to begin our next lecture, I realized that Guiding Eyes staff, instead of preaching to us about the glories of their organization, modeled the patience, tolerance, attention to detail, and respect that they would ask from us; all in all, a good foundation upon which training could begin.

"Today we're going to take you through an obedience exercise that you will be doing every day with your dog while you're here," Eileen explained at the beginning of the lecture. "Dogs are pack animals, and performing this activity every day when you get home is a relaxing way to remind your dog that you are 'Alpha Dog,' the leader of his pack."

Hardly fun or relaxing, I thought, remembering how I had struggled to learn the footwork, hand gestures, and voice commands of this routine. Gradually, though, I had found that this daily time with my dogs created a flow of calming energy between us, which we somehow no longer needed after two or three months. Or maybe I was too tightly wound to accept this gift of relaxation. In any case, I hadn't put Gifford through his obedience paces for five years, and I was nervous when it was my turn to practice the routine with Eileen posing as a docile dog. I attached my leash to a ring on the harness she was holding in her hand.

"Whenever you're ready," she said.

I took a deep breath. "Eileen, sit," I commanded. The leash was in my left hand, and the palm of my right hand faced the ceiling. Hearing the sound of butt hitting floor, I told her that she was a good girl.

"Eileen, down." The palm of my right hand descended toward the leash. I heard a slightly larger thump as Eileen lay down, and after praising her good work, I commanded her to sit while tapping my right thigh with my right hand. I heard a slight rustling jingle as she sat, and I told her how wonderful she was.

"You might want to deliver that command more firmly," Eileen suggested from the floor.

After repeating the "down" command, she suggested that we do two sit stays. After checking to see if she was still sitting, I commanded her to "Stay! Stay!" with the palm of my right hand extending toward her. I passed in front of her making sure I didn't step on her "paws," pivoted, walked as far away from her as the leash would allow, and turned to face her.

"Stay! Stay!" I intoned, reinforcing each command by waving my hand back and forth in front of me like a crossing guard. After pausing for a few seconds to be sure that she hadn't moved, I followed the leash back to her and pivoted so that she was on my left side.

"Good girl," I gushed after waiting another few seconds.

"Very nice; let's try that again."

The obedience routine ended with the "come" command. I stepped back several feet while encouraging Eileen to "come." As I kept up a steady praise patter, I walked back to my original position, and then encouraged her with slight leash tugs to perform a circle. When I sensed that she was close to my left leg, I ordered her to sit. "Good girl," I gushed when she obeyed.

"How did I do?" I asked as I detached the leash from the harness.

"Very nice," she said, and I left the room relieved that my disobedience hadn't been mentioned.

After lunch, we piled into two vans that Erik and Eileen drove to a house that Guiding Eyes owns in White Plains, a medium-sized city about thirty minutes north of New York City. This two-story house contained chairs, tables, and sofas; three computers with access to the Internet; a kitchen area with booths where we could simulate eating in a restaurant; and assorted televisions, radios, CD players, and games. Most training routes began and ended at this house, and since Erik and Eileen would be working with twelve students on an individual basis, "hurry up and wait" was an important part of the experience.

Our main purpose there that day was to do the "Juno walk" to give instructors the chance to continue to figure out which dog would be best for which person, dependent upon the pace we walked, the amount of pull we could handle, and our lifestyle. To accomplish this, they resumed their roles as canine humanoids, holding on to a harness breast strap as we held onto the handle. They walked at varying speeds, veered around obstacles, and bombarded us with questions.

"What are the most important things you need from a dog?" Eileen asked as she veered around something.

I told Eileen that I needed one that walked fast and had a strong pull. I explained that I lived in Washington, DC, and visited New York City, so it should be able to handle loud noises and chaos.

Eileen slowed her pace. "How often do you anticipate working your dog?"

"Every day."

She sped up. "What will you be doing during a typical day?"

"I live alone and walk to neighborhood stores and restaurants. I also use the DC and New York City subway systems to go to office buildings where I lead or participate in meetings and training sessions."

I was slightly breathless at the end of the walk due to the unfamiliar environment, Eileen's constant chatter, and my wanting to prove that I was the Super Dog-Handler of the Universe.

"How did I do?"

"Nice job!" she said, the harness jingling in her hand.

Upon our return to Guiding Eyes, I checked my e-mail using JAWS, ate dinner, and attended the second nightly lecture, which focused on the lives of our new companions prior to meeting us. Eileen and Erik explained that after spending ten weeks in a kennel with his or her mother, each puppy is placed in a home of a "puppy-raiser," where he or she remains from fourteen to sixteen months. While there, these puppies learn basic obedience skills. As time goes by, puppy-raisers begin heeling these "puppies-in-training" across streets, up and down stairs, on and off buses and elevators, and past loud noises and enticing smells. Those dogs who can handle these differing environments return to the Guiding Eyes kennel for four to six months of training. During this period, they learn the key commands: "forward" (start moving), "hop up!" (go faster), "steady" (go slower), "right right" (look for something on the right), and "left left" (look for something on the left). They learn how to work around obstacles that they might face as they assist their blind handler in getting from place to place. They learn to stop at each curb or set of stairs and wait for their handler to give further instructions. They learn to guide their handler into buildings, as well as on and off elevators, escalators, buses, subways, and trains. Only those dogs who survive this training without being stressed out are ready to be matched with a blind handler.

Eileen and Erik cautioned us not to worry if the dog that we would be matched with seemed distant at first, as transferring his or her loyalty from one person to another might be stressful. Other dogs might greet their new handler at first sight. They stressed the importance of taking the experience one day at a time, a good thing to remember as we experience change or encourage others to break a bad habit.

Then the instructors hid away to determine which of the eighteen available dogs would be matched with each of the twelve students. Meanwhile, many of us attended a group counseling session to assist each of us in grieving for our old dog and prepare for the new one. Several students were with their dogs when they died, and one had waited for more than a year before he felt ready for a replacement. I talked about how I was about to pick up Gifford's harness for the first time when I realized I couldn't remember his name.

"I felt so foolish standing on a DC street with a Guiding Eyes instructor while cars zoomed past," I explained. "I knew his name wasn't Dunbar who I had retired the previous day. And of course I couldn't just say 'forward' because the dog's name must always precede the command. So

I'm standing there and the only name that came to mind was Daniel, the infant son of friends from New Hampshire. I finally had to ask the trainer for his name.

"The good news," I continued after the supportive laughter had died down, "is that the deaths of my prior dogs have not been painful because I did most of my grieving when I retired them." Indeed, Gifford's death due to cancer in September 2007 would cause only a twinge of sadness.

My thoughts turned to my new dog as I got ready for bed. Would it like me? Would it be able to adjust to my urban bachelor lifestyle? And would it, like Heidi the Weimaraner, insist on dominating the entire universe, or, like Gifford, be content to rule just a small portion?

And it occurred to me just before falling asleep that encouraging us to give and receive comfort from each other supported us to prepare for the future while bringing our class together.

CHAPTER TWO:
THE NEW DOG
~
MARCH 3–5, 2005

An excited buzz filled the air during breakfast as we speculated about which dogs we would be receiving that afternoon or reminisced about our old dogs. After we finished eating, each of us tried out the obedience skills learned the previous day with a "practice dog" chosen from those who were in training to be guide dogs. Their purpose was to serve as substitutes for the dogs we would be receiving, thus allowing instructors to test their decisions developed during their prior night's discussions. The black Lab I was given was the most disobedient dog I had ever worked with. An instructor told me that he was looking out of the picture window and glaring at other dogs instead of going through his paces. I hoped that my new dog wouldn't be as ornery.

After another Juno walk, lunch, and quiet time, we all came together to learn which dog had been assigned to each of us. While I had gone through this process four times in the past twenty-six years, I couldn't wait to meet my new dog. Before meeting my first dog, an instructor had told me that it was a Weimaraner.

"A what?" I had squawked.

"A Weimaraner."

"What's that?" I had asked, thinking that this must be some sort of joke, as I had never heard of such an exotic breed.

"You'll find out!"

When the instructor ordered me to encourage the dog to come to me, I realized that I didn't know its name.

"Her name is Heidi," he had told me.

"Heidi, come," I had said uncertainly.

I heard her saunter over, and after running my hand through her coat, I commented that she felt like a dachshund. "I won't have to groom her!" I had declared happily, but during the next several hours, she had ignored my efforts to befriend her, tried to jump on the bed, peed on the floor, and spent half the night howling whenever another dog barked. My next dog, Nan, had spent her first hours with me trying to climb on my shoulder and lick my face. As I waited anxiously to hear about the dog to be assigned to me now, I recalled how her tongue seemed to wash my entire face with one swipe as her body vibrated with excitement.

"Peter," Erik intoned, "your dog is a male black Lab named Jules; J-u-l-e-s, Jules."

"Jules!" I repeated to myself, trying to cement the name into my soul. It was easy to remember Nan's name, as she shared my mom's first name. Dunbar was harder until I connected the name with the last name of one of Frank Zappa's drummers.

After the meeting, we each went back to our rooms to wait to meet our new dogs.

"Peter, please meet me in the lounge," Erik said over the PA system, "and bring your leash."

"You know what to do," he encouraged me when I arrived.

"Jules, come!" I said with my heart beating faster than normal.

I heard him saunter over. I held on to his leash and ran my hand over his sleek coat as he turned his head toward other dogs and the instructors who had trained him. Suddenly, he leapt into my lap.

"Hi, Jules," I said as calmly as I could.

"He finally noticed you," an instructor said as others laughed.

Several minutes later, I held onto Erik's left elbow and heeled Jules to my room. Jules spent the rest of the afternoon pointing his head at the closed door, jumping on my lap, rolling on his back, sniffing every inch of the room, and trying to begin dog-wrestling matches with my roommate's dog. Two hours later, he scarfed down two cups of food, and when given the chance to go to the bathroom, I heard him munching ice from a storm drain.

During the evening lecture, he sprang several times out from under the chair in which I was sitting. "Jules, down!" I hissed, trying to wrestle him back to where he belonged. Other dogs were almost as unruly, with one whining because she couldn't get to Eileen and Erik, who had trained her and the other dogs in the room. Meanwhile, Eileen stressed the importance of praising our dogs whenever they went to the bathroom in the area designed for this purpose. She explained that this was important so they would learn to "get busy" on command during fixed times.

As Eileen described the correct way to put the harness on our dogs, I reflected that it was remarkable how learning could take place in the midst of misbehaving dogs and distracted dog handlers, especially since Erik interrupted with suggestions concerning how to encourage our dogs to behave better. Somehow, though, most of us were able to retain much of the information, due to the instructors' calm voices, sense of humor, self-confidence, flexibility, their ability to communicate clearly both to us and each other, and the knowledge that they would have other chances to convey this information.

Back in the room, I began calling family members as Jules slept on his dog bed.

"Hi, Mom!" I announced. "It's a big black male Lab named Jules!"

"Jules," she said, "like Jules Verne?"

"Yes. He's bigger than Gifford and a bit thinner. He has been rather hyper today."

She laughed. "You're used to that."

While waiting to fall asleep, I was startled by the silence surrounding me. After puzzling about this for a while, I realized what I was missing: Gifford's lusty snores.

"Good morning; it's six a.m.," Erik purred over the PA system the next day. "Time to park, feed, water, and park your dogs."

We rolled out of bed, threw on whatever clothes we could find, retrieved our dogs from their beds to which they had been tied the previous night, and heeled them outside. Once in the park area, each of us encouraged our dogs to step off of a curb and to go to the bathroom. Because they didn't understand why we were making them stand around, we had to shake off our grogginess and encourage them to "get busy" instead of greeting each other, sniffing the air, eating ice out of the gutter, or gazing into the distance. Erik was with us to provide guidance and encouragement, as well as alerting us to when our dogs peed or pooped. Over time, instructors would teach us how to determine when our dogs were relieving themselves through subtle signals sent through the leash and what "bathroom actions" were being performed by gently touching their backs. Later on, we would learn how to pick up the poop using a plastic bag as a glove.

"Number one for Jules," Erik called after ten minutes. "You can take him inside."

"Good boy, Jules!" I boomed, relieved that he hadn't followed in the footsteps of my first two dogs who took nearly thirty minutes to go to the bathroom. I heeled him back to my room, attached him to the place where he would be fed, grabbed a dog bowl from under the sink, and headed down to the end of the hall to get the dog food. In order not to run into fellow students, I walked down the right side of the hall to the room where the dog food was stored while announcing my arrival, waited my turn to reach the large plastic garbage can where the food was stored, poured two cups of kibble into the bowl, announced my departure, and returned to my room, this time on the left side of the hall. An instructor was there to assist with the choreography and communication.

"Here you go, Jules," I said, placing the bowl in front of him. He shook himself loudly, wagged his tail against the wall, and devoured his food. After he drank some water, I again took him outside to park, as the stimulation of food and water prompts some dogs to want to relieve themselves.

"It's seven o'clock; time for breakfast," Eileen announced over the PA system several minutes later.

Heeling our dogs to the dining room required communication among students and assistance from Erik, Eileen, or other instructors passing by. "Hold up, Peter," someone might say; or, "Your seat is more to the left." Instructors also assisted us in leaving the dining room, often interrupting their meal to do so.

"It's eight o'clock," Pam announced thirty minutes later. "Time to head to White Plains. Please harness up your dogs and meet in the lobby." Harnesses serve as a signal that guide dogs are in "work mode." Many people have told me how my dogs' bodies have become more rigid and how they become more alert as I put the harness on, and most people understand that dogs shouldn't be bothered when they're working. But neither dogs nor people are perfect.

Six person-dog teams boarded each van under Erik's and Eileen's supervision, and they drove us to the White Plains house. During the next several days, each instructor would be working with six of us one-on-one twice a day between ten in the morning and three in the afternoon to teach us how to work our dogs. Over time, the routes walked would become more challenging, requiring us to cross busy intersections, ride elevators and escalators, walk in areas without sidewalks, and follow our dogs through crowded stores.

Because I was an experienced dog-handler, Jules and I would be at the school for twelve days with an additional five days of training at home. I would be working with Graham, an experienced instructor who understood what I needed in a dog as he had played a pivotal role in building my relationship with my third dog, Dunbar, during a training trip in New York City.

"In 1994, I was still new in guide work," he had told me later. "I was assigned to work with you, probably because the other instructors thought that I could keep up with you. I soon realized what working with a confident fearless traveler was like. Dunbar and you walked at a pace that I didn't think was possible. As I watched the two of you zoom through the city, I realized that I needed to find a way to get your attention as the normal calling out of 'stop' would not work.

"In most situations, I only needed to follow since you knew the city and you were relaxed with your dog. However, there would be times when you would make an error or not judge a clearance accurately. I finally opted to give the backpack that you were wearing a tug when an error was about to occur. This seemed primitive and hardly any technique that I had learned during my apprenticeship, but somehow it worked. I didn't have to shout at you in the midst of the Manhattan mayhem; I just jogged up behind you and gave the backpack a tug.

"You went with it, and we experienced few problems on that New York City trip. I learned two things then: guide work would always involve thinking outside of the box, and that you and I would remain longtime friends."

~

As I heeled Jules out of the White Plains house in preparation for our first training trip with Graham, I wondered what he would do when I asked him to go "forward" for the first time. Heidi the Weimaraner had moved out with such force that I had nearly fallen over. Nan the chocolate Lab and Dunbar moved quickly but with less of a pull, while Gifford moved out more slowly.

"Jules, forward," I said with what I hoped was the right blend of friendly authority, and he moved out briskly, thanks to Graham's familiar presence.

My training routine began to differ from that of my classmates. While everyone else worked their dogs around the block once in the morning and once in the afternoon under the supervision of an instructor, Graham and I worked Jules through two longer training trips, crossing noisy streets and weaving through a maze of people, snow banks, and other obstacles. "Nice job," Graham said at the end of each trip. "Good boy, Jules, good boy!" I gushed, bending down to ruffle his fur. He snorted and shook his head.

In between those training walks, Jules and I joined the controlled chaos as my classmates and I offered our dogs water and gave them the chance to park under Pam's watchful eye. Several minutes later, instructors showed us how to fit our dogs under or near one of the house's restaurant-style booths so they would be out of the way of human feet. They then served us lunch with the assistance of a couple of volunteers, which we tried to eat while chatting with the people at our tables. Many of us had to put both food and conversation aside to persuade our dogs that they needed to stay where they were instead of crawling toward their canine colleagues or into the aisle.

"Time to head back to the school," Eileen called several minutes after the last person-dog team had completed its afternoon trip. I stuffed the braille magazine I had been reading into my backpack, encouraged Jules to stand up, and joined the crowd of chattering classmates as we shuffled to the vans trying not to bump into each other. Once again, six person-dog teams boarded each van under Erik's and Eileen's supervision, and they drove us back to the Guiding Eyes campus. "Time to feed, water, and park your dogs," they reminded us as the vans pulled into the driveway.

As Jules slept on his dog bed after eating, drinking, and peeing, I called my dad to tell him about the new dog. Instead of asking a barrage of questions, he seemed strangely subdued. When I asked him what was wrong, he told me that my stepmother, Pat, was likely to die in a day or two.

"What do you mean?" I squawked. I knew that she was in the hospital due to breathing difficulties, but I thought she was recovering.

"She has taken a turn for the worse," he said, hiding his feelings behind a wall of grumpiness. "You may have to leave Guiding Eyes for the funeral."

Shocked, I stammered an apology and disconnected after asking him to let me know how things were going.

Standing alone in the room, I thought about my evolving relationship with Pat. She was one of the only people who knew each of my prior guide dogs. Heidi the Weimaraner and Dunbar, my third guide dog, stole food from her plate when her back was turned. Nan the chocolate Lab swam in her backyard pool, and Gifford's rumbling snores often served as background music during our conversations.

We met for the first time when I was twelve years old while returning with Dad from a New York Mets game. Mom and Dad had divorced a year earlier, and I didn't want a stepmother. It was more fun to laugh at the way she spoke, "dahling" instead of "darling" and "clahms" instead of "clams," and to play with Tarzan, a yippy Chihuahua who barked when someone moved their hand, rang a bell, or opened the refrigerator door. But Pat had begun to make a dent in my defenses by feeding my sister, Jenny, and me huge portions of stuffed clams, steaks, lamb, duck, salmon, crab cakes, potatoes, pasta, apple pie, and chocolate cake. She had taken us to amusement parks, Broadway shows, and sporting events. While I had appreciated her generosity, I had failed to see her specialness. However, several of my high school and college lady friends had.

"That's not funny," they would chide whenever I made fun of her accent or caused her Chihuahua to bark just for the fun of it. "Your stepmother is really cool." I would mumble something to save face.

After graduating from college, I became interested in writing pop songs, but only the music because my junior high school poetry usually prompted criticism and low grades from teachers and ridicule from classmates. Pat had volunteered to serve as my lyricist, and while we never became pop stars, we did write some good material, some of which was performed in Boston at New England Conservatory of Music and Berklee College of Music. Over time, I grew to appreciate her creativity, sense of humor, and her willingness to try something new.

Several years later, Pat had read articles connected to my pursuit of my MSW onto cassettes so my schoolwork could get done and had given me fresh insights on the issues I was wrestling with. After graduating, I embarked on my career assisting groups and organizations in working across boundaries to accomplish something worthwhile, and again Pat was there listening to my successes and frustrations; asking provocative questions in a disarming way; sharing experiences from her life as a diplomat's wife in Venezuela, Lebanon, Afghanistan, and India; and gently suggesting different ways to address the small but annoying challenges I faced. She also loved my dad and me despite our undiplomatic utterances and dislike of vegetables.

"It's five o'clock; time for dinner," Eileen announced, interrupting my thoughts.

I asked myself whether I should leave Guiding Eyes to be at Pat's bedside. *No,* I decided, confident that she would want me to continue bonding with Jules. I chose not to alert the staff; it didn't feel right to burden them unnecessarily. Instead, I left a message on Jenny's voice mail warning her of Pat's worsening health and joined my classmates for dinner.

As Jules sniffed the air during the 7:30 p.m. park time, I told Graham about his unruly behavior during the previous evening's lecture. Graham told me that he had been pretty mellow when they had worked together. "Yeah right," I snickered to myself as I heeled Jules into our room, but then remembered that both Heidi the Weimaraner and my third guide dog, Dunbar, appeared to be well-behaved introverts until I brought them home.

"Have you never been mellow?" I crooned, parodying Olivia Newton-John's sappy voice of the mid-1970s. He had just peed during the 10:00 p.m. park time, and we were both getting ready for bed. "Have you ever tried?"

Jules grunted.

At six o'clock the next morning, Eileen announced quietly that it was time to start the day.

Today's my birthday, I thought to myself as I heeled Jules to the park area. As he prepared to "get busy," I smiled, thinking about the high points of birthday celebrations growing up: the time when I rode my first roller coaster designed for adults; the time when Mom surprised me with a hi-hat for my growing drum set; the time that I rolled a strike during a visit to a bowling alley from between my legs with my back toward the pins; and the birthday that was nearly canceled due to an ice storm but was wonderful anyway because it was the last time that Mom, Dad, and I were happy together. Dad had moved out of the house one year later, and the divorce became final a year after that.

"You can take Jules in now," Erik said after he had peed and pooped.

As I headed down the hall to get Jules's breakfast, I thought about how my birthday celebrations were much quieter after I graduated from college: small gifts, telephone greetings from family and close friends, and perhaps a special meal with Dad and Pat. As I heeled Jules to breakfast, a part of me hoped that my birthday would be recognized, but it felt wrong to share the news; after all, Guiding Eyes had already given me a great gift, and I didn't feel much like celebrating because of Pat's battle to stay alive.

All such thoughts were forgotten as I immersed myself in the details of the day: putting the harness on Jules and heeling him into the van, keeping him sitting during the trip to the White Plains house, heeling him out of the van and up to the computer room on the house's second floor so I could keep up with my e-mails, encouraging him to remain under the table while eating lunch, and focusing on our two training trips.

During these trips, Graham maintained a steady stream of chatter from three feet behind us warning me about upcoming intersections, obstacles, and other challenges; explaining why Jules was slowing down or veering instead of walking in a straight line; describing buildings, plant life, and other landmarks; and alerting me to subtle mistakes I was making. "Peter," he said, "you are moving your feet before you give Jules the 'forward' command. If you continue doing this, he will learn to look at your feet as a cue to move ahead instead of waiting for the voice command."

Meanwhile, I was enjoying Jules's brisk pace and the nice weather. While trying to absorb Graham's chatter and implement his suggestions, my primary focus was to begin learning how to follow Jules and continue building the bond between us. "Good boy!" I declared at every available chance. When we returned to the house, I ruffled his fur and told him that he was the best dog in the world. At the end of our afternoon walk, he snorted and shook his head as he bounced from foot to foot and nibbled on my finger.

"He's bonding to you," Graham said with a smile in his voice.

Then there were more details: heeling Jules out of the house and into the van; keeping him sitting during the return trip to the school; heeling him out of the van to our room; feeding, watering, and parking him; heeling him to dinner; and trying to keep him lying under the table while eating a meal of vegetable lasagna and garlic bread. Midway through the meal, I noticed the room becoming quiet.

"Happy birthday to you," people started singing from the direction of the kitchen. "Happy birthday to you." The singing grew closer. "Whose birthday is it?" a couple of students called while others joined the singing. "Happy birthday, dear Peter; happy birthday to you."

"Thank you, thank you," I said, pleased and embarrassed.

"We bought you an ice cream cake," Eileen said, placing it in front of me.

"Thanks so much, guys," I said, truly touched. Jules leapt to his feet and shook himself. "Jules, down!" I commanded. As I wrestled him to the ground, I asked Eileen to cut the cake and pass it around to students and staff.

"How old are you?" a student asked.

"Forty-eight," I grunted, still trying to make Jules stay under the table.

After the evening lecture, I returned to my room, attached Jules to his doggie bed, and fell asleep, only to be jarred awake by a ringing phone. It was my stepmother, Pat.

"Happy birthday," she said in a hoarse, tired voice, and then she told me how much she was looking forward to meeting Jules. I told her how happy I was that she was still alive and talked about our adventures together. "Don't worry," she said. "I'll see you when you get home."

At 7:30, Eileen prompted us to park our dogs, after which many of us fell asleep, only to be roused by the 10:00 p.m. final call to park. As Jules and I stumbled into a gusty freezing wind, I reflected that significant change results in significant exhaustion.

CHAPTER THREE:
PLAY DAY

~

MARCH 6, 2005

On Sundays at Guiding Eyes, harnesses are left in the closets, no lectures are scheduled, and many students catch up on sleep. I was looking forward to the arrival of three friends later that afternoon.

Before then, though, I needed to take part in two supervised activities. The first, individual play time with our dogs, had been instituted because many dog handlers either undervalued the importance of play or didn't know how to play with their dogs. This wasn't a problem as I had spent countless hours during elementary school throwing tennis balls, sticks, slippers, and anything else I could find for Suzie, our first family dog.

"There's a high fly ball deep to left field," I would shout as I threw the ball as high and far as I could. "Suzie goes back, back, and makes the catch!" She would dash back with the thrown object and drop it in front of me, hopping from foot to foot as I searched for it. If I couldn't find it quickly enough, she would pounce on it, shove it toward me, and continue dancing until I found it. "Good girl!" I would shout as I threw it for her again.

Suzie was used to being the only dog in the house, and Molly's arrival disrupted her routine. Every morning, both dogs would rush into my room with wagging tails to say hello and to bicker about who would occupy the sun spot. "Peter," Mom would shout over the din, "are you all right in there? Are you getting dressed?"

"Yes!" I would shout, disentangling myself from the dogs.

As Jules and I waited outside of the "play room," I thought about another part of the not-knowing-how-to-play problem: many of us who were raised while blind were discouraged from playing with sighted children because we might get hurt while inconveniencing those around us. But I was lucky. Mom had encouraged me to run around on my own as we walked on the Cape Cod ocean beach and splashed between sandbars during low tide on the bay beach. My sister, Jenny, had taught me how to catch a ball after the first bounce. As I grew older, my classmates had allowed me to take part in kickball, soccer, football, basketball, and baseball games, even bending the rules to allow me to participate on a more equal footing. I was best at kickball. On defense, I could "pitch" the ball to the "kicker" if someone put me in the right place, and on offense, I was allowed to kick the ball without it being pitched and run around the bases either with a sighted person or by myself if I knew the layout of the area. I spent many hours messing around on makeshift basketball courts and fields with neighborhood kids where I learned how to dribble, shoot, tackle, and bounce off tackles. I also swam breast stroke competitively for two summers, and I received the National Rifle Association's Sharpshooter medal with the assistance of camp counselors who helped me align a .22-caliber rifle with a paper target.

But I spent many hours alone on the sidelines when the neighborhood kids decided that I was too much of a burden. Kids would occasionally hit me with spit, slap me and run away, or throw things at me, confident that I couldn't respond to something I couldn't see. Mom had drilled into me that I couldn't use my blindness as a crutch, and over time, I grew to understand these attacks as part of the rough-and-tumble world of boys in which I wanted desperately to take part.

It was much more difficult, however, to accept that my friends would allow me to win an athletic event by only pretending to compete. "You know that the kids allowed you to win that race, don't you?" Mom, my sister, Jenny, or a friend would ask several hours after the neighborhood kids had cheered after my supposed victory. I spent many lonely hours after these false triumphs trying to figure out which success was deserved and which was not.

During my freshman year of high school, I joined the junior varsity wrestling team. I had read about how blind people had successfully wrestled against sighted people, and thought that I had handled myself pretty well during impromptu matches with my sighted friends during junior high school. While I had enjoyed the horseplay and locker room banter, it had become harder and harder to learn the proper footwork and holds, and many of my teammates had been wrestling since seventh grade. I had competed in two tournaments but had been pinned midway through each match. I attended a week-long wrestling camp the following summer, and while the coaches had been supportive, I became uncomfortable with, and amused by, the violence that simmered just below the surface: the taunts, objects being hurled at walls, the careless tampering of personal property, and the constant howl of foul language. I had rejoined the junior varsity team my sophomore year, but my heart wasn't in it. Freshmen were pinning me during practices, and during our first scrimmage, somebody had pinned me five times during a six-minute match. Shortly afterward, Mom told me that I had to drop one of my after-school activities because my grades were slipping. "Fine," I had grumbled, secretly relieved that I could blame her for "forcing" me to quit something that ate away too much of my time, energy, and self-confidence.

$\sim$

WHEN IT WAS OUR TURN to play, I heeled Jules into the room where the lectures usually took place, and Erik handed me a twenty-foot piece of rope.

"I'm sure you know how this works," he said.

"Actually, I don't; this is new."

It turned out that this activity involved attaching that rope, known as a "long line," to Jules's collar, sitting on a couch, and throwing something for him to retrieve. Ideally, the person throws something. The dog runs after it, picks it up, and returns it to the person who cheerfully shouts "Here!" while reeling the dog in with the leash.

Unlike my family pets, my prior guide dogs were lousy retrievers. Heidi the Weimaraner would run in the opposite direction from which an object was thrown to chase rabbits and squirrels. My third dog, Dunbar, would abandon the chase if he saw a chance to steal food, and my other dogs would ignore the thrown object or, after picking it up, run away with it. I therefore didn't think that this activity would go according to plan.

And I wasn't disappointed. The toy box had several items to tempt our dogs. Jules enjoyed chasing after a hard rubber ball, even bringing it back after playing a bit of keep-away first. After several throws, however, he left the ball where it was and sniffed around in the toy box for another option. He selected a "Kong," an object that would bounce erratically when thrown. But this toy did not hold his interest either, so back he came to investigate. We selected a fuzzy object in the shape of a Frisbee. This worked well for a few throws, but he preferred to play tug-of-war instead of retrieving it. The final item in the box was a tennis ball, which held his interest the longest. However, after fifteen minutes, the toys were scattered throughout the room for Erik to retrieve as Jules and I, energized and amused, left the scene.

After lunch, I took part in the second required supervised activity: the obedience routine learned during the first two days. All went well until the first "down stay." I checked to see that Jules was still lying down, praised him for his obedience, ordered him to stay, walked in front of him being careful not to step on his paws, pivoted, and walked as far away from him as the leash would allow. When I turned to face him, he jumped up and shook himself.

"Jules just got up to greet another trainer," Eileen informed me from across the room.

I sighed as I followed the leash back to him. "No!" I exclaimed while giving him a quick "tighten-and-release" snap of the leash, known as a "leash correction." I commanded him to sit and then to lie down, and we successfully completed the obedience routine. Shortly afterward, my first visitor arrived.

"Hi, Peter!" called a familiar voice from a door across from where I was sitting. Elaine had greeted me in that same rich, musical voice since I was three years old. In kindergarten and first grade, she had spent an hour with me nearly every day to teach me to read and write braille, tie my shoes, and other tedious tasks. She had also sharpened my sense of direction.

"Peter," she had ordered as we stood together in a narrow, quiet school passageway, "walk straight ahead."

I obeyed.

"Stop!"

I stopped.

"Turn ... left."

Confused and frustrated, I stood still, knowing I shouldn't go straight, but uncertain which way to turn.

"Turn ... left!" she had repeated.

I guessed.

"No!" she had said when I had turned in the wrong direction. "Turn ... left."

So that way is left, I had thought as I turned in the correct direction.

"Good!" she called. "Walk straight ahead."

Again I obeyed.

"Stop!"

I stopped.

"Turn ... right!"

Gradually, I had guessed less, and by the time I was six, I had learned how to distinguish right from left.

Jules sprang out from under the chair in which I was sitting. He shook himself and wagged his tail. His paws skidded on the tiled floor as he tried to drag me across the room. "Hi, Elaine!" I called. I stood up and tried to rein him in.

"He's quite a handful." Elaine and I laughed and hugged as Jules continued to prance. "Where's your husband?" I asked.

"Ed will be here soon once he finds a place to park."

"Control your dog," Eileen called, trying to keep from laughing.

"You're very handsome," Elaine told Jules, "but it's too soon for me to play with you. You need to listen to Peter."

After Jules calmed down, we walked to the Coffee Room and settled into two plastic chairs across from each other. "I'll send your other visitors in when they arrive," Eileen said from the doorway.

"Thanks," I called over my shoulder. "Jules, down!" Grunting loudly, he sank to his haunches and fell asleep as Elaine and I began chatting about what was new in our lives: her work with developmentally disabled children; my professional exploits; her social life with her husband, Ed, a jazz drummer; my social life with my DC friends; the love lives of her two adult sons.

"Are you seeing anyone?" she asked.

The question caught me off-guard even though she usually asked about my love life whenever we talked.

"Nothing new," I said, hoping to change the subject. Over the years, I had told Elaine that while forming friendships with women was easy, converting them to romantic relationships was a mystery I hadn't solved. I didn't go on many dates during high school and college, but I usually found a partner to join me at proms and other important parties. Finding a date in college was harder because there were twice as many men as women on-campus, and the combination of schoolwork, music activities, and weekend parties left me little time to worry about competing in an area where I felt outclassed. How was I supposed to know if a woman really liked me or was just being nice because I was blind? And if I couldn't be confident that she liked me, how could I think about sex, especially since most people seemed to believe that we blind people either weren't or shouldn't be interested in something so "dirty." My male college buddies would leave their dates with me during parties, telling me that I was one of the few people they trusted to keep their partners entertained without trying to make a move. *If they only knew,* I thought wryly, remembering the technique I used to explore forbidden parts of a girl's body while in high school. When a girl with a sexy voice offered me her elbow so we could walk somewhere together, my hand would veer toward a more interesting part of her body. "Peter," she would squeal as others around us laughed, "that's *not* my elbow!"

My first romantic fling took place at Guiding Eyes during the summer after I graduated from college. While building a relationship with Heidi the Weimaraner, I bonded with a fellow student who was in her late twenties. We compared notes about our experiences learning to work with our new dogs as they lay by our feet. We took part in raucous card games. We laughed and talked together for hours about my life as a college brat and her life in a working-class neighborhood in Brooklyn, New York. We spent an afternoon with Elaine, leaving our dogs behind because an instructor had told us that we weren't ready to work them away from the school. We engaged in romantic horseplay with our clothes on, not caring about the wagging tongues of students and staff. After leaving Guiding Eyes with our dogs, we spoke regularly by phone, and six months later, she visited me in my studio apartment in Yonkers, New York, where she helped me lose my virginity. The experience was vaguely unpleasant because of the half bottle of Scotch we had drunk, and because we had been jarred awake several hours later to the sound of her dog whining and the smell of half-eaten kibble that Heidi had vomited up four feet from where we were sleeping. Three months later, she was engaged to someone else, and I had moved to Boston to begin working toward my master's in music.

My second major romantic fling took place at Guiding Eyes seven years later. While adjusting to the exuberant ways of Nan the chocolate Lab, I began hanging out with a fellow student who was seventeen years old. We supported each other as we adjusted to our new dogs. We took part in raucous card games. We talked quietly about my experiences in the music industry and her life as a high school senior in Birmingham, Alabama. We spent an afternoon with Elaine, this time bringing our dogs along. We engaged in romantic horseplay with our clothes on, not caring about the wagging tongues of students and staff.

After leaving the school with our dogs, we spoke occasionally by phone, and one year later, we met again at the annual Guiding Eyes Walkathon. During this joyful chaotic event, up to one hundred graduates and dogs joined with puppy-raisers, local Boy Scout troops, and other dog-lovers to walk fifteen kilometers to raise money for the school. After walking the route during a torrential downpour, Elaine, Ed, and my sister, Jenny, had driven us and our soggy dogs to Guiding Eyes and helped us dry them off. After the noisy celebratory post-walk meal featuring the smell of one hundred damp dogs, we had spent an hour alone together rolling around half-naked on a hotel bed as our two dry dogs slept on the floor. Three months later, we had lost touch.

"I've sort of given up on looking for the right person," I confessed to Elaine. "I'm happy living alone. I'm not very good at dating, and if it's meant to be, it will happen."

"I understand," she said with a tinge of sadness. "Ed! We're in here!" she called toward the door.

The tags on Jules's collar jangled as his head shot into the air and his body vibrated with excitement. "Stay!" I said, putting my hand on his head. To my surprise, he obeyed.

"Hey, Elaine. Hey, Peter. Sorry it took so long!" Ed called. He strolled to where we were sitting, grumbling about the lack of parking. "We brought you this," he said, handing me a large heavy jar. Jules sprang to his feet and began sniffing every inch of its surface.

"Jules, down!" I ordered, giving him a leash correction. "Thanks," I said to Elaine and Ed in the most normal tone I could muster. Jules sat, his head pointing to the jar. "Jules, down!" I repeated. He sank to the floor with a grunt, his head still in the air and his tail slithering back and forth across the floor. "Good boy," I said, ruffling his fur. "What's in the jar?" I asked, placing it in the middle of the table.

"A mixture of sweet and salty goodies," Elaine explained. "We thought you might need a snack once in a while. And happy birthday!"

"Thanks. I'll share it with my fellow students."

"He's quite a handful," Ed said as Jules fell back to sleep.

"Not as crazy as Heidi," Elaine and I responded, and we were off reminiscing about her antics during her first year with me: how her boundless energy caused Mom's golden retriever to collapse in exhaustion as she barked in exasperation; how the only way to control her exuberant greetings was to hand a guest a glass of water.

"She hated getting wet," Elaine said. "I held that glass of water toward her, and she sat right down with her eyes fixed on the glass."

46

"I'll never forget hanging out at your place listening to Ed's band rehearse," I said. "I was relaxing on your couch drinking a beer as Heidi wandered about the room. All was fine until I became aware that the trombonist's solo was weird. He played two notes, stopped for three seconds, played six notes, stopped for five seconds, played four notes, and then just stopped playing." Elaine and Ed started laughing. "Then Elaine walked over, dragging Heidi by her collar, and told me she had to stay with me for the rest of the rehearsal. When I asked why, she explained that Heidi had been standing in front of the trombone player and swatted the slide with her paw whenever he tried to play."

"And what about the time at that small Manhattan night club?" Elaine said. "We were sitting at a table listening to Dave Frishberg sing his quirky songs. Heidi was lying under the table with the leash attached to your leg."

"And then all of a sudden you asked me to rescue you from my dog," I said. "I thought she was still lying down. But then I noticed that her leash had gone slack and that it led under the table to you."

"She had crawled under the table inch by inch like a marine begging for food at nearby tables along the way," Elaine remembered, "and next thing I knew, she was trying to climb into my lap."

A voice cut through our laughter. "Hi, Peter." Again, Jules's head shot into the air. "Stay!" I said, putting my hand on his head. "Hey, Eric, come in," I called as Jules settled back down. "You remember Elaine and Ed from the walkathon?"

"Of course," Eric said, strolling over to greet them. "You might want to stay by us," Elaine suggested. "Jules is very excitable."

"Good idea," I said, not relishing another battle of wills.

"Hi, Jules," Eric said from across the table. Like Elaine and Ed, he understood the importance of guide dogs learning to focus on their handlers instead of nearby temptations. "I'll talk to you later." Jules's tail thudded several times on the floor.

The conversation veered to the annual walkathon: the usually clear and crisp weather, the greasy burgers, and the joyful chaos. We laughed about how I walked too fast for people to keep up with me, and talked about how my mom, my sister, Jenny, Elaine, and Ed, who came to the event almost every year, had met some of my other friends there. We told Eric about Heidi's antics at the walk: how she howled throughout a recording of the "Star Spangled Banner"; how she leapt onto a picnic table after completing the walk for no apparent reason; and how she would engage in long conversations with Mom, using her large repertoire of sounds to get her point across.

"But you didn't know Heidi," Elaine said to Eric after another round of laughter.

"No," he said. "The first of Peter's dogs that I met was Nan."

"That's right," I agreed. "You invited us to your apartment for dinner and to meet your wife and kids—"

"And she started tearing around our two-bedroom apartment—"

"Sliding all over the tile floor—"

"Scaring my little girls—"

"I know," I said a little defensively. Elaine laughed. "But she was friendly."

"Yes, but she was big and brown and full of energy," Eric explained.

"And she was nine years old; it was our last trip together before heading up to Guiding Eyes the following morning so that I could begin my new life with Dunbar."

"But why did you retire her?" Eric asked.

"She had been slowing down during the past year, she had arthritis in her back legs, and I was traveling a lot as part of my job."

Eric and I began regaling Elaine and Ed with examples of Dunbar's exploits as a food thief: the time he stole a rich pastry that Eric had bought for a friend; the time that he rescued a half-eaten sandwich out of a trash can while we were conducting a meeting; and the time he climbed onto a counter in full view of experienced dog handlers and stole half a cake meant for people to eat.

"And then there was the time that Dunbar disrupted the opening ceremony of a large conference where white males were pretending to be Native American elders," Eric said after another burst of laughter. "We found the event to be both silly and a bit insulting. So we decided to leave, but we didn't want to disturb anyone."

"When Eric nudged me, Dunbar and I stood up—"

"And the three of us shuffled to the aisle without disturbing anyone too much—"

"And as we walked toward the door, Dunbar shook himself—"

"Which totally ruined the atmosphere," Eric concluded.

"It's four o'clock; time to feed, water, and park your dogs," Eileen announced over the PA system.

"And then we bumped into several colleagues a couple of hours later who told us that at least half of the people attending the ceremony had walked out after Dunbar's disruption," I said.

Still laughing, we said our good-byes, and Jules leapt into my lap.

CHAPTER FOUR:
BACK TO WORK
~
MARCH 7–9, 2005

As Jules and I walked together to our room after sitting through a morning lecture, I was pleased with the bond we were building between us. He had quickly peed and pooped at six in the morning. We had gently but enthusiastically played together on and around the bed before breakfast. He had slept peacefully while I ate and during the lecture. We seemed ready to take our next step toward conquering the world.

And then Jules suddenly stopped. He stood stock still while I tried to figure out why he had stopped and what I should do about it.

"It's me," Graham called as he walked down a flight of stairs to my left.

I sensed Jules's head gently moving back and forth, and wondered if he was trying to figure out which of us was his master. Six months later, we ran into him at the annual walkathon, and Jules barely wagged his tail. But our relationship was still in the embryonic stage after only four days together.

"He's having a brain fart," Graham declared. We both laughed, breaking the spell, and Jules and I walked the rest of the way to our room.

During our two White Plains training trips, I began learning how giving Jules treats increased his concentration as we maneuvered through pedestrians, cars, slushy snow banks, and other clutter. Guiding Eyes had recently added "treat training" to its toolbox because treats speed up the learning process while encouraging dogs to focus more on their handler instead of distractions around them. As Graham taught me the basics, I realized that I had unwittingly used this technique while walking on a Cape Cod beach with my mom and Heidi the Weimaraner. As soon as we took off her leash, she would run so far away that she appeared to my mom as a small gray dot. Instead of coming when called, she chased seagulls, rolled in horse manure, ate dead fish, or barked at anything she considered to be in her territory. Mom had suggested that I give her a piece of kibble whenever she came when called, and soon she began charging toward us every few minutes, poking my back left pocket with her cold wet nose and barking if I didn't give her a treat quickly enough.

During the last portion of our afternoon trip, Graham dropped back from his usual three feet behind us to half a city block to see how Jules and I would work together without him, and we completed the route flawlessly. I would be leaving the school in five days, and we needed to learn to function as a team before we left.

Overnight, a windy rain storm moved in, and neither students nor dogs looked forward to walking out of our rooms at six o'clock the next day for "park, feed, water, and park." Like many of the other dogs, Jules tried to step onto the curb and out of the rain. "No! Off! Get busy!" we pleaded. "Good boy, Jules!" I said when he finally peed, and he darted up on the curb and into the room, spraying me with water on the way.

Each dog has its own way of working in wet weather. Heidi the Weimaraner would howl as I dragged her into the rain, but once she understood that she had to get wet, she would assist me in arriving at a dry destination, pawing the ground when a traffic light didn't change quickly enough, and poking pedestrians out of the way with her nose. During our morning White Plains training trip, Jules increased his speed, but with the exception of grazing a couple of poles, his work over a one-and-a-half mile route was flawless.

During lunch, I heard the instructors frantically whispering in a corner, and it became clear that they were revamping the afternoon's training schedule due to worsening weather conditions. We were told that the training day would be shortened; to save time, they continued, each of us would be paired with someone who walked at a similar pace. They described the approach we would be using and the route we would be taking, announced who would be paired with whom, and encouraged us to communicate with our partners.

However, the driving snow and gusty winds only allowed half of us to take our afternoon training trip. I was one of the fortunate ones, as Jules needed to burn off some energy. My human partner and I plowed through the snow-covered sidewalks with the aid of our intrepid dogs, and Jules celebrated our return with his usual array of snorts, head-shakes, and prances. He even mouthed the leather harness, a definite "No!" as harnesses are both tempting chew toys and expensive.

The trip from White Plains to Guiding Eyes lasted ninety minutes instead of the usual thirty. As Erik drove, I reflected on how our afternoon training trip mirrored the ever-changing business conditions, bureaucratic shifts, and other swerves that we regularly experience. Guiding Eyes leaders encourage their instructors to adapt their training to unforeseen events, a necessity when training a diverse group of people with visual impairments in ever-changing weather conditions and surroundings. Ordinarily, this "working-in-partners" strategy is used later in the program to teach students how to better control their dog's pace, but this weather change prompted the instructors to work together to determine how best to adapt this technique and to communicate it quickly and clearly. The solid relationships they had formed with us during quiet times encouraged us to trust them to lead when the weather turned nasty. And we were all committed to working toward a clear compelling goal.

As Erik continued driving with the radio playing softly and the wind rattling the windows, I remembered my first day at my first job in Washington, DC. Dunbar and I were just about to attend our first staff meeting when John, the organization's president, walked into my office and announced that his administrative assistant was allergic to dogs.

I cringed as New York City taxi drivers used this "allergy excuse" when they didn't want a dog in their car. Sensing my unease, John said that he hoped that this wouldn't be a hardship, but that Dunbar and his assistant couldn't be in the same room together.

I made a quick decision. "No problem; Dunbar can sleep in the office."

"Are you sure?"

"Yes. He doesn't like meetings anyway."

At the meeting, John introduced me to the group and asked me to talk about "your companion who isn't here." I introduced Dunbar: that he was a male black Lab and my third guide dog, and that we had been living and working together in New York City for four years before moving to DC. John told the group that my boss had been working with me over the past several weeks to be sure that I had what I needed. He talked about how they had installed JAWS, a software package that converted the text on the screen from print to speech. He mentioned that a specially trained mobility instructor had assisted Dunbar and me to learn how to walk from my apartment to the office. "What else?" he had asked.

"Well," I said, not sure of the direction of his thoughts but determined to play along, "I had to learn how to use your phone system ... also, how to find the bathroom, water cooler, meeting rooms, kitchen, and the elevators."

"Then I learned five minutes before this meeting that my administrative assistant was allergic to dogs," John continued, "so I had to work with Peter at the last minute to find a solution that was all right for Peter, my assistant, and of course, Dunbar."

John then reminded us that the organization's mission was to work toward resolving the most heated conflicts, and that planning was important, but that something unforeseen almost always took place at the last minute. "Call it the Dunbar Factor," he suggested as some of us chuckled quietly. "And the way we handle those last-minute Dunbar Factors can make the difference between success and failure."

"We're here," Erik announced, turning into the driveway and shutting off the engine. As another gust of wind bounced snow off of the windows, we sighed in relief as our dogs shook themselves; we had survived a Dunbar Factor and couldn't wait to escape the weather into our rooms to unwind.

Jules leapt out of the van and dragged me into the building. "Peter," Graham called from across the lobby as his feet skidded across the tile floor, "let's go into the Campbell lounge and see how he reacts to doggie boots." These boots are designed to save dogs' paws from the slush, salt, and heat reflecting from the summer city sidewalks, but Jules resisted having his feet covered, stepping out of one boot as I tried to put on another. After a ten-minute struggle and many dog treats, however, his feet were covered, and after heeling him around the lounge for a couple of minutes, he was walking at his usual brisk pace.

The daily obedience routine followed the removal of the boots. Since he seemed sluggish, Graham and I decided to find out if holding a treat in a strategic location would galvanize him into action.

"Jules, come!" I commanded.

He sprang into action. He jumped. He pranced. He twirled. He snorted. He bowed. He shook himself. He wagged his tail. Then he sat down. Graham and I howled with laughter as I gave him his treat despite the fact that his bravura performance had nothing to do with the "come" command.

After dinner, I received two phone calls. The first came from several visually impaired male friends who took time from their weekly boys'-night-out get-together at a local DC pub. Gifford and I had helped organize this event and almost always took part when we were in town. These bonding sessions over burgers, potato skins, fried mushrooms, onion rings, fried pickles, and beer was a highlight of my week, and I relaxed as we bantered over the phone about workplace frustrations, romantic gossip, and my progress with Jules.

"It's 7:30; time to park your dogs," Eileen called over the PA system.

"Got to take my dog into the tundra," I groused, "but we'll see you in a couple of weeks."

The second call came as I was attaching Jules to his dog bed. It was from Dad, who informed me that my stepmother, Pat, was expected to leave the hospital in ten days. While I was relieved to hear about her recovery, the dissonance between this news and his prior prediction of her death was jarring. "Jules will amuse her," I said to myself as I fell asleep.

The following morning, all dogs received boots because of the salt-covered yet icy sidewalks. Controlled chaos reigned as students, instructors, and dogs vied for space on the floor to practice putting boots on dogs who didn't want them. Most dogs were more hesitant to walk, sit, or lie down with their boots on, and all of us were relieved when they were removed.

However, the dogs were less than pleased when we put their boots on again, but soon realized that the "I'm pathetic" act would not save them from having to do their jobs. While Jules's pace gradually became less jerky during our two White Plains training trips, one of his boots fell off twice, something I wouldn't have noticed if Graham hadn't been around. *These boots might save his paws from the slush, salt, and heat reflecting from the summer city sidewalks*, I thought, *provided they stay on his feet*.

During the afternoon trip, Jules and I crossed numerous streets, avoided all stationery objects, and lightly bumped into one person. Toward the end of the trip, I asked him if he thought Jules and I would be ready to go home in three days.

"Absolutely!" he said without hesitation.

Buoyed by his confidence, I heeled Jules upstairs to a comfortable chair in a quiet part of the house so I could continue writing the Reuters America Reverse Mentoring Program report. I had been working on this document since Jules had sauntered into my life. "Jules, down!" I commanded, positioning his body so that his head would be facing in front of the chair in which I was sitting. "Good boy," I said, ruffling his fur.

Jules sighed contentedly as I took my Braille Lite out of my backpack and placed it on my lap. I turned it on and began summarizing the successes of the program. Many members of the Leadership Team were establishing informal mentoring programs within their business units and had committed to serving as mentors. Policies were being drafted to encourage managers to insure that people from diverse backgrounds were given equal consideration for advancement opportunities. A workshop aimed at reducing stereotypes held about Arabs had taken place. An initiative aimed at recruiting qualified people with disabilities was being put together in the organization's St. Louis office. An internship program aimed at providing work experiences for low-income high school students was being organized. Several senior managers had volunteered to serve on the committee that was driving the diversity initiative ...

The voice of Melinda, the class supervisor, floated up from the first floor, where she was leading an informal discussion with the rest of the class. I turned off my Braille Lite and listened to her describe our progress and mistakes. She reminded us that changing behavior often could be frustrating. "You will have good days and bad days," she declared.

"She's right," I mumbled to myself, remembering a remark that Kenneth, a mentor from Durham, New Hampshire, had made toward the end of a six-day Exploring Group Dynamics program that Nan the chocolate Lab and I had attended in the early 1990's. At the beginning of the program, ten of us had sat nervously in a circle as Kenneth and his assistant explained that we were there to learn how groups form and how our individual behavior affected the process. "But we don't have a group yet," he had said, "and we need to begin to form one. Let's get started."

Over the next six days, we had worked toward forming that group. We talked. We laughed. We shouted. We thought and felt. We struggled. We ate meals together. We complained about the difficulty of the task and how Kenneth and his assistant weren't helping us enough. But over time, we got better at talking with and listening to one another. We learned how to cooperate and address conflicts. By the end of the program, we had formed a closely knit group with wise support from Kenneth and his assistant. Their calming presence had encouraged us to forge ahead. They had inserted observations and encouraging words. They had talked about goals, roles, control, inclusion, affection, authority, and other concepts related to the issues we were struggling with. They had highlighted an idea foundational to Kenneth's work: the difference between doing something for someone so they don't have to do it (which he calls "help") and doing what's necessary so that someone can do the task themselves (which he calls "support"). "Giving someone a fish," he had explained, "is an example of 'help,' while teaching someone to fish is an example of 'support.'" And toward the end of the seminar, he had encouraged us to remember that change was gradual, and that reminding others to expect "good days and bad days" might support them to prepare for the bad days.

I began weaving elements of Kenneth's approach into my work supporting people to change their behavior. Instead of separately lecturing students with disabilities and hiring managers about how to be more effective during the hiring process, I brought both groups together and supported their efforts to learn from each other. Instead of talking at New York City taxi drivers about how to improve their customer service skills, I created a supportive space where cabbies could learn from each other about driving more safely, handling uncooperative passengers, respecting police officers, and working within the laws governing the treatment of people with disabilities. And instead of preaching to executives about the importance of workplace diversity, I developed the Reverse Mentoring Program so they could learn directly from employees from underrepresented groups.

As we dog handlers-in-training laughed at another remark from Melinda, it occurred to me that Guiding Eyes instructors were especially good at assisting us in managing tension, which Kenneth defines as that subtle energy that either helps or hinders us to perform. If levels are too low or high, we appear restless, bored, or paralyzed. Astute leaders, however, can assist in regulating this energy so that those they lead can do their work effectively, and a gifted leader can, over time, support those they lead to continue to perform effectively under increased tension.

Learning to exert authority over an animal of a different species while living with a diverse group of people creates a fair amount of tension, which grows with the increased complexity of the skills we need to learn and the environments in which we work our dogs. Instructors lower tension through humor, a pat on the back, and highlighting the improvements they observe. They raise tension by challenging us to do better, alerting us to our mistakes, and forcing us to figure things out for ourselves.

When Melinda announced that the vans had arrived, the rest of the class began collecting their belongings and moving toward the front door. I turned my Braille Lite back on, anxious to finish this section of the report. I wrote that 70 percent of the mentors and many of the senior managers stated that they would be less likely to explore career options outside of the organization. Noticing that the house was getting quieter by the moment, I quickly added that participants also talked of better communication among business units, stuffed my Braille Lite into my backpack, roused Jules from a deep sleep, and hurried downstairs and out of the front door.

By this time, getting in the van with Jules was routine. I waited for Erik to tell me that the coast was clear. I heeled Jules to the door. I coaxed him to stay put as I stepped up into the van. I prompted him to join me, and together we headed toward a seat.

But his leash became entangled with the leash of another dog. We separated the leashes, and all seemed fine until the person sitting next to me wondered aloud if we had switched dogs. "Impossible!" I declared, but then began wondering if the dog with its head in my lap might be a bit smaller and thinner than Jules. We checked with Graham, who confirmed that we had indeed switched dogs. All was made right, thanks to some complicated ad hoc maneuvering, a good thing since Jules walked *really* quickly and the other dog walked *really* slowly.

Back at Guiding Eyes, Jules flawlessly performed his obedience routine and enjoyed play time chasing that Kong toy, even sometimes bringing it back. As Erik retrieved the scattered toys, he told me that he had noticed that I sometimes couldn't remember Jules's name.

He was right. While these memory lapses rarely happened when the harness handle was in my hand, I would forget his name while heeling him from the dining room to my room or from the White Plains house to the van.

"I have trouble remembering names," I confessed, "and I guess having not fully grieved Gifford's retirement makes it harder?"

"Perhaps, but it's important that you remember the name."

"You're right."

"Jules, the family jewels?" he suggested.

"That might work. Thanks!" I said, remembering the line "this is our family jewels" from Sister Sledge's 1979 anthem "We Are Family." Erik and I laughed as the three of us left the room together.

CHAPTER FIVE:
PREPARING TO LEAVE

~

MARCH 10–11, 2005

The next morning, I once again heeled Jules to the room where another lecture would be delivered. While I wasn't sure I was ready to go home in two days, I was growing tired of listening to familiar material, surrounded by students who I hadn't really connected with. As we entered the room, Jules's vehement bark jarred me from my thoughts.

"What's that about?" I asked. It was the first time I had heard him bark.

"There's a life-sized stuffed dog perched on top of the piano," Erik said as I eased into a chair and ordered Jules to lie down under it. As Eileen described the proper use of a "Halti," a muzzle-like device that makes it easier to get a dog's attention, I felt his head pointing at this intruder.

"The idea behind a Halti is to have full control of the dog's head," Eileen explained. "It creates some counterbalance between the neck and the snout; if your dog's head drops—"

Jules sprang out from under the chair. "No!" I hissed. I gave him a quick "tighten-and-release" leash correction. I ordered him first to sit and then to lie down.

59

"The Halti is like a bridle on a horse," Eileen continued as I slid Jules under the chair, "but it's hard to compare since a dog doesn't have the same shaped head—"

"Jules, no!" I grunted as he again sprang out from under the chair. As I wrestled him to his proper position, Eileen explained that Guiding Eyes only recommends the use of a Halti when a handler doesn't have the strength to control his or her dog without one. "Nonetheless," she concluded, "we want you to learn how to put one on in case you need to use it."

As she walked around the room with the stuffed dog so that each of us could practice putting the Halti on its head, Jules redoubled his efforts to reach it. By the time she came to me, his antics were so distracting that I never got the chance to practice; instead, I gave him a strong two-handed leash correction under Erik's supervision.

"What was he thinking?" I asked after Jules had calmed down.

"No idea." Erik chuckled as he walked away.

During the morning training trip, I worked Jules around the White Plains train station. With Graham's assistance, we practiced getting on and off escalators. This involved me finding the railing with my right hand, stepping on the escalator while encouraging Jules to jump on behind me, waiting until the railing flattened out, and stepping off while encouraging him to jump off behind me. As we rode the escalator, I told Graham that I couldn't use these moving stairways with Heidi the Weimaraner because she wasn't trained to work on and off them. Going downstairs into a New York City subway station wasn't a problem because many pedestrians also used the stairs. But people trying to walk in the opposite direction would complain as we ran up four flights of trash-filled stairs.

"Why don't you use the escalator?" people shouted.

"No! Sorry!" I would yell over my shoulder as we dashed by.

Jules began guiding me around obstacles as we walked the length of two platforms at breakneck speed. "I would love to have been there to see you in action," Graham said, chuckling.

I turned my head in his general direction. "It's so much easier to use escalators," I said, "although it was amusing to get under the skin of those intrepid New York City commuters after listening to customers yell at me all day."

Graham next positioned Jules and me three feet from the edge of the platform facing the train tracks and encouraged me to urge Jules to start walking. My prior dogs when told to go "forward" in similar circumstances had stood still and tossed their heads as if to say, "I will not allow us to fall on the railroad tracks despite what you say." "Good girl," I had told Heidi and Nan when they disobeyed my command. "Good boy," I had told Dunbar and Gifford.

"Jules, forward!" I said in my most authoritative voice, expecting him to react like my prior dogs. Instead, he disobeyed my command by making a sharp left turn and dragging me down the platform. "Good boy!" I said, trying to conceal my surprise. After catching my breath, I asked if he had responded properly, and Graham explained that they had recently taught the dogs this new approach to improve the safety of both dog and handler.

Guide dogs see things that their visually impaired handlers cannot. They are constantly evaluating options and choosing the simplest and safest path, and safety trumps obeying their handlers. Those dogs that successfully complete guide dog training learn to create a "safety zone" for themselves and their handlers, and develop strategies to move away from objects that invade this zone. When a dog begins working with a new handler, it readjusts this zone based on feedback received. For example, Heidi soon learned that I didn't mind stepping in puddles, and therefore didn't hesitate to lead me through them, so long as I didn't splash her. All of my dogs learned over time that I wouldn't be upset if I lightly bumped a stationery object, but would complain if they ran me into a pedestrian. Thus, "intelligent disobedience" takes place when the handler commands his or her dog to do something that the dog believes will invade their "safety zone," and the handler must trust his or her partner's judgment enough to follow its lead and praise it for its disobedience.

As we walked back to the White Plains house, I thought about how all organizations claim they value "intelligent disobedience." They want their staff to take thoughtful detours from the way they usually do business to provide the best possible service to their customers or to create the next great gadget. However, many managers discourage these "disobedient" actions when they overly punish failure, fail to reward the behavior when it does take place, or use the organization's policies and procedures manual as a sledgehammer. Such actions can cause "malicious obedience," the slavish following of the rules even though the employee knows that doing so will irritate the customer, create a substandard product, or "gum up the works."

While waiting to cross a street, I inwardly squirmed and snickered at my use of malicious obedience while working at that stodgy bank on Wall Street. While the customers and working conditions there were nicer than at my prior job, my first boss pretended not to be at her desk whenever I sought her help.

"You know she is trying to ignore you," a sighted colleague finally said.

"I thought so, but I wasn't sure," I confessed, trying to hide my annoyance.

"Hey!" the colleague shouted a few minutes later, "how would you like to be sued?"

"What?" the manager asked.

"We all can see how you ignore Peter whenever he comes to your desk."

Her denials caused an African American male to state that he had seen the same thing.

"I would never do that!" she shouted. She stalked to my desk. "You don't believe what they're saying, do you?"

"As a matter of fact, I do. You shuffle papers really loudly. I'm not stupid."

She walked back to her desk, and we managed to stay clear of each other until I received a call from an elderly woman who was hard of hearing. Her name was Mrs. Glasscock, and she had the demanding yet pleasant voice of someone used to getting their way. She reminded me of my grandmother who had insisted that we all call her "Pussy" even when her children had encouraged her to choose another name. I had called her every week while in college because she had paid for more than half of my room and board, and I would begin each of these calls with a cheerful "Hi, Pussy." This energized my grandmother while reducing my roommates to fits of uncontrollable smothered laughter.

As Mrs. Glasscock and I began to talk about a complex issue with her account, a bank rule flashed through my mind: always use the person's name instead of "yes, sir" or "yes, ma'am" because, we were told, it would always make the customer feel special. So, I obeyed in a clear and commanding voice that carried throughout the entire call center.

"Yes, Mrs. Glasscock! … I'm sorry, Mrs. Glasscock! … I understand, Mrs. Glasscock! … Here's how we'll solve the problem, Mrs. Glasscock!"

As the conversation continued, I became aware of more and more colleagues enjoying the diversion. "What's her name?" a male voice asked with suppressed laughter. "Don't be too hard on her!" a female coworker purred in my ear. I heard the muffled footsteps of several colleagues approach my desk, pause, and walk away.

"Is there anything else I can help you with, Mrs. Glasscock?"

"Oh, no. You've been so kind."

"Thank you for calling, Mrs. Glasscock. Have a nice day."

The room was silent when I hit the disconnect button and began writing a summary of the problem with her account. As the volume of the room returned to its normal hum, my boss stood over my desk.

"What was that all about?" she snapped.

I continued writing and suggested that she look at the screen. She approached my left shoulder, stood still for a few seconds, and shuffled away.

My coworkers became more relaxed around me after that call. It became less important that I was blind and used a weird-looking gadget that allowed me to read the information on the screen in braille. I began to be included more in the chitchat and banter that made the work more tolerable.

But I knew that my patience with the bank was running out after a confrontation with my new boss. It all started with a call from a customer who wanted to know the value of her account. After she gave me her account number, I asked her for the names on the account.

"What do you mean?"

"What are the names on the account?"

"What do you mean?"

All I needed to do, I knew, was to ask for the caller's name to insure that I was giving the account balance to someone legally entitled to it. However, I also knew that the bank "script" mandated that we ask "what is/are the name(s) on the account?" and I had heard fellow employees being publicly reprimanded for not following this procedure. I also disliked my boss, who spent more time blathering about the wedding dress she intended to buy instead of assisting us in resolving customer complaints. And I was fairly certain that I was about to be laid off even though managers assured me I was one of their best employees.

"I need to know the names on the account," I said to the caller.

"What do you mean?"

"What are the names on the account?"

"I don't understand what you're asking."

"I'm sorry, but I really need to know the names on the account."

"Ask for the customer's name!" screeched my boss from across the office.

"What is your name?" I asked into the phone, and the caller gave me her name and Social Security number. I gave her the account balance, thanked her for calling, and hung up. Within seconds, my boss had summoned me into her office.

"I want to play back the tape of that call," she had said as Nan the chocolate Lab stood next to me, "because you were rude to that customer."

"I know."

"What? You knew you were rude?"

"Of course! You know that bank procedures require that I ask 'What are the names on the account?' You made that very clear during our initial training, and I have heard you and other managers criticize us when we don't follow the script!"

"But everyone knows rules are made to be broken. Why do you insist on following them so rigidly?"

"Because I believe that both you and the bank think that following the script is far more important than being polite to customers!"

My boss, Nan, and I left her office, and we did our best to avoid each other until she left the bank to join her fiancé in Germany. I left six weeks later to begin my pursuit of an MSW.

~

THE AFTERNOON TRAINING TRIP FEATURED "traffic checks" designed to find out how Jules and I would react when a car invaded our "safety zone," a common occurrence in urban areas. As we began crossing a street, a car screeched by in front of us. Jules jumped back, keeping both of us safe, provided that I followed his lead.

"Good boy, Jules!" I boomed.

"Don't you know how to drive?" Graham shouted.

"Enjoy the rest of your trip!" cackled Melinda, the class supervisor who had pretended to run us over.

Jules performed flawlessly during the rest of the trip, meaning that he recovered quickly from unpleasant surprises. However, slippery sidewalks prompted him to walk faster. Heidi the Weimaraner had insisted that we jog together down icy New York City sidewalks, scattering pedestrians as we went.

"Can't you slow down?" they would shout.

"No!" I would shout over my shoulder, as all attempts to slow her down resulted in my sliding along the ice on my backside. Fortunately, Jules did slow down upon request.

Back at Guiding Eyes, we met Shanon, the instructor who would be working with us for five days in Washington, DC. While Jules, who recognized her because she also took part in his training, barked, whined, snorted, and twirled to get her attention, I described several long routes that I hoped we could familiarize Jules with during our time together. She reminded me that dogs, like people, can be overstressed, and encouraged me to keep Jules under good control until her arrival.

The next morning, everyone ordered their dogs to remain sitting while staff heeled other dogs through the room. Contradictory commands bounced off the walls. "Stay!" each of us implored as the new dogs sauntered past. "No!" many of us shouted when our dogs stood to greet these new visitors followed by the snap of quick "tighten-and-release" leash corrections. "Good boy!" some of us cheered when our dogs remained at "sit" as we offered them dog treats. Over time, the sounds of cheery voices and canine treat-crunching overpowered the irritated voices and leash corrections as our dogs paid more attention to us than the visiting dogs.

We boarded the vans after the obedience activity and headed to a local mall where each of us worked our dogs through and around shoppers and other obstacles with little space to maneuver. Back at the school, we all gathered for a "photo shoot," first as a group and then as individuals.

I dislike posing for pictures because the process is humiliating and the final product is irrelevant. After getting into proper position through trying to follow a barrage of confusing directions from well-meaning parents, teachers, or friends and enduring pokes and prods, I am told that I must smile. I cannot see the picture, but have to listen to criticisms about my ineptness as a picture poser. But I tried to hide my impatience as Eileen placed Jules and me in the proper position.

Once in place, I joined my fellow students in ordering our dogs to sit. While most of the dogs sat most of the time, they swiveled their heads from side to side to look around them instead of facing the camera. Finally, everybody was properly positioned.

"Okay," piped the photographer. "Smile ... on the count of three! One—"

"Jules, sit!" I hissed.

Chaos erupted as instructors and the photographer made silly sounds to attract the dogs' attention.

"Let's try this again!" piped the photographer as the instructors tried to keep the dogs focused on the camera. "One ... two ..."

"Over here!" he pleaded, trying to get a dog's attention. Meanwhile, I checked to see if Jules was sitting.

"Good boy," I mumbled.

"Face this way!" the photographer barked.

"Who, me?" I asked, startled.

"Not you," Erik said as Eileen adjusted another student.

"Okay!" again chirped the photographer. "One ... two ... three!" We all held our breath. "Looks good!"

We cheered as the dogs stood and shook themselves.

"Hold on!" the photographer shouted. "I need another picture!"

After the second group photo, each of us posed for individual pictures, which were temporarily posted on Guiding Eyes's website, embedded in a photo identification card for us to carry in our wallets, and given to us and to the puppy-raisers who raised our dogs prior to their arrival at Guiding Eyes. Next, Graham, Jules, and I visited the veterinarian, where I learned that Jules was healthy, that he weighed seventy-seven pounds, and that he was born on May 31, 2003. Then, I recorded a greeting to be included in the video of the graduation ceremony that would take place without me eight days later.

This ceremony recognizes students' successful completion of the training. The moment can be especially significant to those who become blind as adults, as learning to partner with a dog is sometimes their first major achievement since becoming blind. Stephen Kuusisto, in his 1998 book *Planet of the Blind,* writes about his journey into blindness and how getting his first Guiding Eyes dog helped propel him from a homebound hermit to a married and successful author, professor, and disability activist. Another student lost her vision due to diabetes. After graduating with her first dog, she went back to school and received a master's degree in communications. She is currently a sought-after motivational speaker and is the first certified therapeutic riding instructor in America who is blind. Another graduate became blind due to a rare eye disease, and reports that her first dog has made it easier for her to perform her job as a sommelier and purchasing agent for a major retailer. She is working toward receiving a master of wine certification, which requires eight years of intensive study. "Guiding Eyes for the Blind gave me my life back," she wrote on their website. "My dog has opened many doors for me that I couldn't have passed through without him ... The school is the single most important thing in my life—it's my lifeline."

The Guiding Eyes graduation ceremony features speeches and songs from students and staff, presentations of gifts from students to instructors, and occasional barks, whines, grunts, and more physical activities from our dogs. At an earlier ceremony, I had reached down to retrieve the leash of Nan the chocolate Lab after a fellow student and I had finished performing a song. The leash was not where it was supposed to be, and as I continued searching, I noticed laughter mixing in with the applause.

"Don't worry, we've got things under control," boomed the director of training. He handed me the leash.

"What happened?" I whispered to another instructor as she led Nan and me back to our seat.

"The two dogs started their own version of the World Wrestling Federation smack down toward the end of your performance."

"Oh," I said sheepishly. As the ceremony continued, I sat down and quietly commanded Nan to lie down under the chair.

So while I dislike ceremonies, I regretted that I would miss this one, as I remembered the sharing of humorous stories, the celebration of the community that students and staff had created, and the lack of condescension that we visually impaired people face whenever we are recognized for accomplishing something that seems ordinary to us but superhuman to those who can see. These warm confidence-building events are the exact opposite of a ceremony I attended at a large government organization aimed at honoring their outstanding employees of the month. While my boss had recommended me for this honor, she had told me she was too busy to attend. So I had arrived alone and sat by myself. The unit head, after arriving ten minutes late without an apology or explanation, had doled out plaques in a bored, robotic voice as fellow award-winners dutifully applauded. When my name was called, Heidi the Weimaraner had guided me swiftly down the left-hand aisle, but instead of leading me to the unit head, she had turned left and led me out of the room.

"You're going the wrong way," the unit head's voice had hissed through the static of the PA system.

Snickering to myself, I heeled Heidi back into the room, received my plaque, and worked her back to the call center.

"How was the ceremony?" my boss had asked as I passed her desk.

"Okay, I guess," I had mumbled without slowing down. "It was good not having to deal with angry customers for a while."

Back at my cubicle, I had slam-dunked the plaque into the wastebasket, where it landed with a satisfying *plunk*, sat in my chair, took a deep breath, and answered my next call.

And I was also sorry that I would miss the chance to meet Jules's puppy-raiser after the Guiding Eyes ceremony. An employee of the school notifies puppy-raisers when the dogs they have raised have been matched with a person, and invites them to attend when it becomes clear that the match will be successful. Puppy-raisers drive for up to ten hours from New England, New York State, New Jersey, Pennsylvania, Maryland, Virginia, and North Carolina to meet the new dog handler and to see the dog in its professional guise. After the graduation ceremony, puppy-raisers are invited to introduce themselves to their dog's new handler, causing the dog to strain to be reacquainted with their prior caretakers. But harnesses must be removed before the real reunioning can begin.

We dog handlers are equally excited to meet these remarkable people who are willing to nurture a dog for eighteen months or longer and then release it into the hands of a stranger. I have been fortunate to meet two of these families: the Steenburgs, who raised Nan the chocolate Lab in upstate New York; and the Burketts, who raised my third dog, Dunbar, in northern Virginia. Both families were brimming with stories about these dogs' inquisitive nature, their silly antics, and strategies they used to keep them under control.

"Dunbar needs constant stimulation," Riva told me as he whined for her attention. "He was a real terror around the house until someone invited both of us to tour an airplane. I was terrified that he would trash the plane, but he behaved like a champ as he took in all of the sights, sounds, and scents of this new environment. After that, I got him out into the community every day, and he settled right down."

The puppy-raisers leave after a couple of hours, often with a new puppy from the Guiding Eyes kennel to raise, while we continue our lives that are enriched by their sacrifice.

After completing the video greeting, Graham, Jules, and I made a quick trip to Guiding Eyes's "obstacle course" where Jules and I worked around a variety of objects of differing sizes, shapes, and heights. All went well until we encountered an obstacle that completely blocked our way. Jules veered off the sidewalk, worked around the obstacle, but decided to blaze a trail in the snow instead of bringing us back to the sidewalk.

An hour later, I headed to dinner, leaving Jules in the room alone; I wanted to be sure that he wouldn't do anything naughty while I was gone. While at dinner, I thanked the instructors for their support.

"That family jewels thing worked. Thanks," I told Erik.

"Just relax and allow Jules to do the work," Graham suggested.

"And don't walk so fast," Melinda quipped as we reminisced about how she had jogged after Gifford and me around Washington, DC, while supporting us to become a team.

After dinner, I walked alone to my room and stood outside straining to hear any noise from Jules. Hearing none, I walked into an intact room and greeted him. He stood up, shook himself, and wagged his tail. Then it was time to pack the collars, a "tie-down chain" that would allow me to attach Jules to a sturdy piece of furniture, a five-pound bag of dog food, a six-month supply of heartworm tablets, and other equipment that Guiding Eyes provides its students.

Then, Jules and I headed to the Coffee Room so that I could say good-bye to some of my fellow dog handlers-in-training over a couple of beers. As I chatted with two veterans of the Vietnam War, two college students, and a housewife, Jules and another dog crawled toward each other on their bellies until their noses touched.

"Jules, no!" I shouted, but too late. Both dogs began snorting and rolling around together with tails thumping. "Jules, come!" I commanded, followed by the snap of a leash correction. "Stuart, come!" echoed the handler of the other rowdy dog. Seconds later, all was quiet except for the sound of panting dogs.

"I think it's time to remove one of the mischief-makers," I said. Jules shook himself as we stood up. While feeling around the table for my empty beer bottles, I discovered the jar of treats Elaine and Ed had given me several days earlier. Noticing that it was still half-full, I told the other people in the room that I would be leaving the jar behind. I retrieved the beer bottles and dropped them into the recycle basket near the door.

"And tomorrow we really are going home," I told Jules as I heeled him to our room. I was relieved that I had survived this phase of the training, and nervous because the real work of teaching him to work well on my home turf would now begin. I was also confident, having molded four guide dogs to meet my needs … and Shanon, the home instructor, would join me in three days.

Heidi talking; October, 1988

Peter, his fellow classmates, and their dogs; taken in the Peter
Campbell Lounge at Guiding Eyes for the Blind; March, 2005

Peter and Jules; taken in the Peter Campbell Lounge
at Guiding Eyes for the Blind; March, 2005

PART II:

HOME TRAINING

CHAPTER SIX:
HOME ALONE WITH JULES

~

MARCH 12–13, 2005

"Good morning. It's 6:00 a.m.," Erik purred over the PA system. "Time to park, feed, water, and park your dogs."

For the last time at Guiding Eyes, Jules and I headed outside, where he quickly parked in three inches of snow. Once inside, I showered, dressed, finished packing, and ate my last Guiding Eyes meal. And for the last time, I attended the morning lecture.

"Just saying good-bye and good luck," I called from the door, interrupting Erik's flow.

"Jules's Slip Collar is on wrong," he said as he strolled over to shake my hand.

During a lecture four days earlier, Erik and Eileen had given each of us leather collars. They had asked us to replace the Slip Collar with these new collars before dinner and switch back to the Slip Collar before breakfast the next morning. They explained that the leather collars were safer since the links on the metal collars could, in rare circumstances, entangle with the collars of other dogs or objects. I had made these collar changes flawlessly during the past four days, but my luck had run out.

"Great," I mumbled to myself as the rest of the class chorused their good-byes. I fumbled to fix the problem.

"The collar's still wrong," Erik intoned.

"Are you ready?" Pam the instructor's assistant called from the hallway.

"If I can get this stupid collar on right."

"Here, let me help," Erik said. He fixed the collar.

"Thanks. Good-bye. Good luck!" I shouted over my shoulder as I walked with Pam to a Guiding Eyes van. Their responding good-byes faded into the distance as we settled in for the hour-long ride to LaGuardia Airport.

While Pam drove and chatted with another instructor, I reflected on the diversity of my fellow students. We lived throughout North America. Our views concerning hot-button political issues ranged widely and were rarely discussed.

But there were similarities. Each of us wanted to develop a strong working relationship with our dog. None of us worked full-time. Three of us were of retirement age, one of us was attending college, and another was planning to move to Germany to marry a military man. The rest of us, however, experienced the same challenges that other blind people face while trying to get and keep a job: unavailable, unreliable, or overcrowded public transportation; an overworked network of state vocational rehabilitation agencies set up to assist us in finding jobs; and the sense that most sighted people, while well-meaning, don't believe in our abilities. Each of us shared stories of incompetent uncaring VR counselors. We grumbled about jobs we had lost due to down-sizing, inept bosses, evolving job responsibilities to which we could not adjust, and fewer chances to move ahead. We also talked in more subdued voices about how mismatched clothes and skills, laziness, and poor hygiene sabotaged our efforts. Like other special-interest groups, we spend too much time focusing on how others are throwing obstacles in our way instead of acknowledging how we contribute to the problem and connecting with others to find solutions.

About 1.8 million people who are legally blind live in the United States. According to the Social Security Administration, the unemployment rate among visually impaired people is somewhere near 70 percent. Most of the blind people I know who are employed assemble products in specially designed "sheltered workshops," fill dead-end jobs for the government, or perform social services or legal work in agencies serving people with visual impairments. During the past five years, many organizations employing blind people have begun grooming some of their workers to fill management positions, and several are led by blind people. Very few people with visual impairments work in corporate America.

~

AT THE AIRPORT, PAM LED Jules and me from the raw, windy outdoors into the warm, dry terminal. As we stood in line waiting to go through security, Jules's head swiveled from side to side as the chaos swirled around us. The metal in his harness made the metal detector beep, so security personnel had to hand-scan him. This proved futile because he sniffed everything in sight, whirled, and shook his head, all while wagging his tail. When the wand-waver finally allowed us to pass through, we headed to the gate with laughter from airline employees, security personnel, and passengers in our wake.

At the gate, I asked the ticket agent if I could sit in a bulkhead seat because there would be more room for Jules to stretch out on the floor under the seat. Because the flight was only half-full, the agent also blocked off the seat next to where I would be sitting so we would have more room. When it was time to board, I gave Pam a quick one-handed good-bye hug and held onto the elbow of an airport employee so he could assist me down the jet way and onto the plane. A flight attendant showed me to my seat, where I put my luggage in the overhead bin. I sat down, helped Jules lie down under the seat, and fastened my seatbelt.

During take-off, Jules abruptly sat up, quivering slightly, but settled down a minute later.

"Is he all right?" a flight attendant asked as she handed me a ginger ale.

"He's fine," I assured her. "It's probably his first flight." He spent the rest of the flight amusing the flight attendants by poking their lower legs with his cold nose.

When the plane pulled into the gate at Reagan National Airport, I followed a routine that I had perfected over the years: grabbing my backpack from the overhead compartment, stuffing my belongings into it and slinging it over my shoulders, lifting my suitcase down from the overhead compartment with my right hand, picking up the dog's harness with my left hand, and encouraging him or her to lead me "forward" off of the plane, trying not to bump into other passengers. Like my other dogs, Jules shook himself and vibrated with excitement as he led me off the plane. Since this was our first day alone together, we weren't ready to zigzag through the maze of chattering passengers and other obstacles, ride down an escalator, and head outside to the taxi stand without help. As we waited for assistance from an airline employee, Jules lay down with a grunt. "Don't worry," I told him, "we'll be zooming through this airport soon enough."

When the cab arrived, I settled into the front seat with Jules sitting on the floor and his head in my lap for the twenty-minute ride to my apartment. "You sure know how to win friends and influence people," I told him. He sighed as the driver chuckled. While I was enjoying his good-natured enthusiasm, I was concerned that his attempts to dominate his surroundings might distract him from guiding me safely from place to place while annoying those who were not dog-friendly.

After Jules failed to christen his new park area near my apartment building, we rode an elevator to the sixth floor and walked down a long hall to my studio apartment. Three objects dominated the twenty-by-twelve-foot space: a sofa across from the door and under a window; a twin bed on the left wall; and a large computer desk on the right side. The entrance to a tiny kitchen was across from the entry door, and the bathroom could be entered by walking through a closet.

I allowed Jules to explore this space on leash. His first discovery was the dog food container across from the kitchen, which he sniffed enthusiastically. His second discovery was the basket of dog toys near the sofa. Soon, he was chomping on a bone while attached to the sofa by a tie-down chain as I unpacked and went through e-mails. When I lay down to take a nap, he placed his head on my leg.

As we jockeyed for position on my twin bed, I smiled, remembering the ritual that Heidi the Weimaraner insisted on following. Every night after I got into bed, she would slither headfirst under the covers, complaining shrilly if I didn't give her enough room. I would wake up several hours later as she squirmed out of the bed, shook herself, and drank some water. She would then come back to the bed with water dripping from her muzzle, this time slithering bottom-first under the covers.

After the nap, Jules devoured his dinner, drank some water, and used his park area for the first time. Then the obedience routine, more play time, and one more chance for him to "get busy."

As he slept on a rug attached to the sofa, I wondered if he missed his canine colleagues: the one who ate ice instead of parking; the one who slept so soundly that he was difficult to get moving; and the ones he roughhoused with despite our best efforts to keep them focused on their work. While I was happy to be sleeping in my bed after being away for twelve days, I missed the controlled chaos and joyful noise of the Guiding Eyes community.

After Jules peed and pooped at his new park area at seven a.m. the next morning, I worked him around the block, a route I had walked daily since I moved to DC. However, as this was his first time working this route, I had to focus on details: go to the corner; turn right and cross Twenty-Fourth Street making sure the light was in our favor; turn right and walk to a set of stairs preceded by a gradual incline; encourage Jules to go up the stairs and past a set of whirring escalators; turn right shortly afterward and walk to the corner; turn right and walk to the next intersection; recross Twenty-Fourth Street, again making sure that the light was in our favor; and turn right and encourage him to turn left into my apartment building, the entrance of which was located between two sets of hedges. Back inside my apartment, I talked to him about his brilliance as I filled his food and water bowls. After tying him to the sofa, I called the front desk to ask for someone to come fix my clogged toilet.

Jules was silent when the handyman knocked on the door, a good thing since guide dogs are not supposed to bark in order not to bring undue attention to the dog or its handler. However, Heidi the Weimaraner barked while running free in fenced-in backyards. She barked when she wanted something, once declaring on a Cape Cod beach that she wanted the sandwich of a stranger. Oboists and trombonists were subject to indignant barks, as were people who spoke too softly or loudly when walking past the Manhattan apartment we shared.

Nan the chocolate Lab barked once with her harness on: to trumpet the arrival of a bank vice president who was preparing to tour the call center where I worked. Off-harness, she barked when someone knocked on the door but would greet the arriver with a wagging tail and licking tongue. Gifford would usually bark once or twice in a bored sort of way whenever somebody knocked, as if to say, "I know I'm supposed to act like a vicious wolf, but that is *so* not happening. Just open the door so I can greet whoever's there."

After the handyman left, I decided to let Jules wander around the apartment without a leash, rationalizing that he seemed comfortable using his park area and that we had successfully worked our first route together without help from a Guiding Eyes instructor. I was curious to find out how he would respond to a taste of freedom. I knew that Guiding Eyes would be unhappy, but I was the Super Dog-Handler of the Universe. So I took off his leash … and he just stood there.

"You're just gonna stand there and look stupid?" I taunted.

The tags on Jules's collar rattled as he shook his head.

I threw a toy across the apartment. He dashed after it and began squeaking it. After several more throws, I went through my e-mails and made several phone calls, finding it harder and harder to concentrate because of the chomping, squeaking, and scurrying feet as he scattered all of the dog toys around the apartment. But I learned from Linda Walters that Gifford was adjusting to retirement. I talked to my dad, who seemed more cheerful and relaxed as he told me that on St. Patrick's Day my stepmother, Pat, would come home, where she would celebrate her birthday.

During the afternoon, we repeated the route we had worked during the morning, stopping on the way at a local Chipotle where I picked up a fajita for lunch. With the fajita bag in my right hand and Jules's harness in my left, we began our journey home but became entangled in a forest of tables and chairs filled with people eating their lunch outdoors during one of the first warm days of spring. We eventually emerged from the forest, thanks to shouted directions from several diners.

"My fault," I told Jules in the elevator. "I told you to turn right too soon. We'll do better next time." His head turned toward the fajita bag.

After a neighbor and I made a quick trip to the Manhattan Market, a small locally owned grocery store, I gave Jules another chance at freedom. As I went about my business smiling at his antics, I thought about how Jules, like all dogs, was assessing my priorities as they related to him. After all, I was in charge, so he needed to figure out how I reacted to what he was doing. He experimented, and succeeded in getting on the bed but failed to receive any human food when he turned his head toward the fajita bag. His noisemaking garnered a rueful chuckle and a smile, but his prior failures to pay attention during the obedience activity resulted in a firm "no" and a leash correction. Over time, he would decrease those behaviors that caused negative consequences while increasing those that prompt a positive response. However, because he is stubborn and I am imperfect, he would continue to experiment for the rest of our time together. But consistency is key, which is why I need to set and maintain behavioral boundaries, for it is harder to break bad habits than to prevent them from forming.

As Jules and I flawlessly completed our daily obedience routine, I reflected that some of the same principles govern our behavior on the job. Management at the stodgy bank on Wall Street promised to fire anyone who arrived late. They kept their promise, and we learned to arrive on time. Management also rewarded customer-friendly behavior; I once was given a half day off with pay after assisting a customer in resolving a complex problem.

At my first job, though, things were different. When I arrived, more experienced blind colleagues told me about a blind employee who was rude to customers, nasty to colleagues, and gave inaccurate information. And his guide dog wandered around the office, stole food from tables, and signaled the end of the workday with a loud bark. One day, the employee returned from lunch with a bottle of wine and encouraged us to drink with him. At day's end, a blind colleague complained to his boss and was told: "What am I supposed to do? The guy is blind."

While this employee was finally fired, this incident contributed to creating a community of blind employees built on contempt, cynicism, and anger. We ignored, made fun of, or maliciously obeyed management rules. We did our best to sabotage any improvement efforts our bosses tried to put in place, and led the cheers when a supervisor announced at the end of a particularly bad year that headquarters had rated our call center as the worst in the country. As I chained Jules to the sofa, I snickered to myself remembering how I had become distracted while on the phone with a customer when a rude, inept male employee who was both blind and black had shouted, "You bitch!"

"What was that?" asked the customer.

"Please hold." I stabbed the "hold" button as the employee shouted "You bitch!" even louder. "How dare you interrupt me when I'm on the phone!"

"You gave the wrong answer!" shouted a sighted elderly white supervisor who we disliked because of her inept rudeness.

"I don't care, bitch! You should have asked me to put the customer on hold before correcting me!"

"You tell her!" shouted a friend whose boss had refused to allow him to see a nurse after a car had knocked him down as he returned to work after lunch.

"You tell her!" I cheered while howling with laughter. My ex-boss had refused to believe that I had a severe migraine headache for which I was hospitalized for three days.

More and more of us cheered on and laughed at the combatants until the supervisor retreated.

"Go away, bitch!" the employee had shouted at her back.

"They're both morons," I said under my breath as I fought to regain my composure. "Thank you for holding," I said sweetly into the phone, but all I heard was the purr of a dial tone.

CHAPTER SEVEN:
PATTERNING

~

MARCH 14–15, 2005

I was lying on my bed late the next morning idly reading a book on my Braille Lite when Shanon called to tell me that she was on her way. "I'm ready," I told her. I had already walked Jules around the block, dealt with my e-mails, completed an hour-long aerobics routine, and sorted through the mountain of mail that had piled up while I was away with the assistance of a neighbor. But I hadn't eaten breakfast, so I was ready to work Jules to a neighborhood pub to order their meat-lovers pizza.

When Shanon arrived, I hopped off of my bed, padded past Jules, who was sleeping on the rug, and opened the door. After greeting each other, she asked why Jules wasn't attached to the sofa. "You know that guide dogs are either supposed to be with you on leash or attached to something for at least two weeks," she added, "and that you only give dogs more freedom after they have earned it."

"I know," I said sheepishly, for I understood that keeping a dog under control was critical to assure that it would focus on its handler instead of tempting sights, sounds, and smells. I had heard stories of dogs given too much early freedom that destroyed furniture or became ill after foraging food from garbage cans. I had even heard about one dog that had escaped through an open door and had been hit by a car the day after its handler brought it home.

As the silence lengthened, I protested to myself that Jules had behaved very well since our return home. Yes, he had created some good-natured chaos the previous day, and it was true that I had to attach him to the sofa earlier that morning to convince him that barking and pawing me would not allow him to take possession of a ten-pound medicine ball I was using as part of my aerobics routine. But I had released him after my workout, and he had fallen asleep, not even getting up to greet Shanon or the neighbor who had helped me to go through my mail. I could have attached him to the sofa before Shanon's arrival, but that seemed silly since he was so calm; indeed, I thought that she might admire my independent thinking. But I sensed that pleading my case would increase the tension for no good reason, so I mumbled an apology, and we agreed to discuss our plans together over lunch.

At the neighborhood pub, I explained that I hoped we could work Jules to a local Popeyes, a fast-food restaurant specializing in fried chicken; the China Café, a local Chinese restaurant; and the site of the nongovernment organization (NGO) that I was assisting in developing strategies to improve the way they worked with employees and customers with disabilities. I explained that each restaurant was around a mile from my apartment and that each route presented unique challenges.

"I'm not sure that we can do all that," Shanon cautioned, "because it might put too much stress on the dog."

"I understand," I said as Jules lay under the table sleeping through the loud conversations and restaurant clatter.

After the waiter took our order, I asked her how I could tell if Jules was too stressed.

"Excuse me!" Shanon barked, "but you really shouldn't distract a guide dog."

"That's right!" I snapped. I had no idea about what was happening, but the music sounded familiar. "Guide dogs, like police dogs, are working animals and should not be distracted while in harness!"

"Sorry," said an unfamiliar, meek male voice as he disappeared into the din.

Shanon sighed. "People can be so rude."

I sighed back. "What did he do?"

She explained that the man was looking at Jules in a "come here" kind of way, which Jules, being asleep, didn't see.

"I'm glad he wasn't distracted." I told her about how Heidi the Weimaraner would leap to her feet, wag her tail, and shake herself when she decided someone was interested in her.

"So how can I tell if Jules might be stressed?" I asked again.

Shanon said that she wasn't sure, that every dog had its own way of coping. Graham would later remind me that both working dogs and people deal with stress all the time. "This isn't always bad," he explained, "because a certain level of stress will assist people and dogs in concentrating on their work." Stress among guide dogs can be relieved by setting clear expectations, praising good behavior, giving occasional treats as a teaching tool, allowing them to fetch thrown objects or to roughhouse with other dogs, giving them plenty of affection, and allowing them time to relax. When stress is not relieved, a guide dog may become more distracted around other dogs, increase sniffing or scavenging, and be less willing to work. "However," he concluded, "there are so many variables that can be perceived as stress it is difficult to tell which ones may or may not be causing a problem. The best philosophy is to learn your dog's normal behaviors really well, and then to be alert to when he or she moves away from the normal rhythm."

Not so different from managing workplace stress, I thought. Research shows that in order to discourage "bad stress reactions" among employees, managers should set clear expectations, as well as praise and model good behavior. Another stress-reducing strategy is to give cash bonuses, gift certificates, or time off for outstanding work. Allowing employees to connect with their colleagues, a rough equivalent of "dog play," can allow staff the support they need to get over the rough spots. Discouraging these healthy outlets will likely result in more employee whining and growling and less focus on getting the job done. Graham's final piece of advice is also sound: really talented leaders learn the most effective work rhythms of each person they lead and find ways to restore those rhythms that stress disrupts back into harmony.

~

AFTER LUNCH, WE BEGAN TRAINING Jules to guide me from my apartment building to Popeyes. I was initially edgy about submitting to Shanon's scrutiny, as I was an experienced dog-handler on home turf and was still smarting from her calling me out on my not attaching Jules to that sofa. Over time, though, I relaxed because much of the route, while long, was simple: a right from the apartment building to the corner of Twenty-Fourth Street and Calvert Street; turn right and cross Twenty-Fourth Street; continue down Calvert Street to Connecticut Avenue, a six-lane street with lots of traffic; cross Connecticut Avenue when the traffic on Calvert Street started moving; and continue down Calvert Street, crossing a small bridge and two quiet streets until arriving at an intersection where three streets merge at weird angles. Jules and I jumped at the chance to stretch our legs and enjoy the sunny, brisk weather while Shanon called out encouraging words and friendly suggestions from several yards behind us. After beginning to teach him how to work through that three-streets-at-weird-angles intersection, we continued down the street past a gas station until the next intersection.

"We are now on Columbia Road," I announced over my shoulder after turning left at the intersection. "Popeyes is about halfway down the street just past a large crack on the sidewalk."

But I failed to find the crack, and we shot past the restaurant.

"I see the crack," Shanon said, "but Jules took you around it."

"But this worked so well with Dunbar and Gifford," I half-jokingly complained, knowing that a new dog might handle the same situation differently. We backtracked to show Jules the restaurant door.

The return trip to my apartment was going smoothly until Jules started slowing down.

"He has to park!" Shanon called from behind.

Over time, guide dogs learn to pull their handlers over to the curb when they need to "get busy." Since it was too soon to teach Jules this trick of the trade, we guided him to a spot on the street where he pooped while Shanon shielded him from oncoming traffic.

At my apartment, I attached him to the sofa, where he drank some water and slept. After Shanon left, I also fell asleep only to be jarred awake by a telephone call from Mom wanting to know how things were going. As I described our adventures, Jules stood up, shook himself, and barked shrilly.

"Was that Jules?" she asked.

"Yes," I told her. "No, Jules!" I growled over my shoulder.

"Perhaps you might want to look after him?"

"No way! I will not let a bratty dog rule my life!"

When our conversation ended several minutes later, I walked over to find Jules standing still with his head fixed in my direction.

"Hi, bratty dog," I said as he stretched out on his front legs as his backside quivered in the air propelled by a fast-moving tail.

After Jules devoured his dinner, I called Susan, a nurse from North Carolina who had raised him with the help of her husband and three children. "He must have been a challenge," I said, "since he is a large hyperactive lap dog with an independent streak."

She laughed and told me that she had been sure that he would make a great guide dog because loud noises and other surprises never fazed him. She confessed that her seven-year-old son had encouraged him to lie on his bed. "I hope that's not a problem?"

It was my turn to laugh. "Don't worry; I'm used to having dogs sleep on my bed."

I told Susan that we were well on our way toward making a successful team, and that I appreciated Jules's independent spirit since it countered my stubborn streak. She said that she had heard good things about our work together from Graham but was surprised about his hyperactivity. "He was pretty laid-back when he was with us," she said.

"It's still early; he might settle down over time."

After again thanking her for her hard work, I hung up the phone.

"Time to park," I told Jules. I went to the sofa, but he wasn't there.

"Jules?" I called.

No response.

"Where are you, you silly Labrador?" I wandered over to my bed and found him sleeping on my pillow.

After a good night's sleep, Jules and I were ready to roll. His harness was on, his tail was wagging, and my left rear pocket was full of "Charlie Bears," little morsels we would be using to encourage him to be a better student. "Hey, Peter," Shanon called as Jules guided me out of the elevator and down a carpeted ramp toward her. "How did things go last night?" I described how he had been forcing his head between my legs and trying to squeeze his body through while bowing, snorting, and wagging his tail, and I tried to thwart his progress while muttering endearments and drumming on his hindquarters.

"Silly dog!" We laughed as we headed out the door toward Popeyes.

"Oh yes," I said after I had worked Jules across Connecticut Avenue, "and his most recent approach to retrieving is to chase after the squeaky, pick it up, leap on the sofa, and roll around and snort while squeaking the toy as loudly as possible."

When we arrived at that three-streets-at-weird-angles intersection, Jules stopped at a wheelchair ramp.

"I'm pretty sure that this isn't the correct ramp," I called over my shoulder, "because I don't think we veered far enough to the right."

"You're correct."

I grabbed onto Shanon's left elbow and allowed her to guide Jules and me to the correct ramp.

"Jules, sit!" I commanded while tapping the top of the proper ramp with my left foot. He sat. "Good boy." My foot kept tapping as I fished in my left rear pocket for a treat. "Take it," I encouraged, moving my right hand in his direction. "Good boy!" I gushed as he snatched the treat from my hand.

"Nice job," Shanon encouraged as she guided Jules and me twenty feet in the direction from which we had come. "Okay, go ahead and rework him to that wheelchair ramp."

"Jules, forward!" I commanded, and sensed him veering to the right and stopping at the proper spot.

"Nice!" Shanon exclaimed from three feet behind.

"Good boy!" I enthused as I again tapped the ramp with my left foot, commanding him to sit, and offering him another treat. Shanon next guided us fifty feet away from the ramp. Once again, I commanded him to go "forward," and he again worked flawlessly, earning lavish praise and another treat.

After using this "patterning" technique to encourage Jules to learn to work through the rest of the intersection, we continued our journey. As we approached the restaurant, I felt the crack in the sidewalk that he had guided me around the previous day. I slowed down to alert him that something important was about to happen, and commanded him "left, to the door" while sweeping my right hand to the left. Once again, he missed the door on our first pass. Shanon, however, appeared to guide us to the door, which I tapped with my right hand before offering him more lavish praise and another treat. She then guided us first twenty feet and then fifty feet from the door, and he flawlessly guided me to the proper spot, prompting more praise and treats.

While relaxing in the sun outside of the restaurant, I commented that using treats as rewards increased Jules's focus on me instead of the pigeons, dogs, fawning humans, and other distractions.

"That's the idea," Shanon said.

"But if I gave him a treat every time he did something good, wouldn't he focus too much on the food instead of my voice?"

"Yes, and he would get fat." Overweight guide dogs concern Guiding Eyes because weight gain can cause joint pain, heart problems, and other conditions that might shorten the life of a $50,000 working dog.

"So that's why we're encouraged to give our dogs fewer treats as they become more familiar with the routes they work," I mused, remembering how as a college sophomore I had learned about using food to teach a pigeon to learn something new. As I began working Jules back to my apartment, I described to Shanon how during a lab, as part of a Psychology 101 course, two classmates and I had trained a pigeon to peck at a certain spot. During the first phase of the experiment, my partners first gave our "subject" a food pellet whenever it came close to doing what we wanted as I muttered encouraging words from several feet away. Within an hour, the pigeon was doing what we wanted, receiving a pellet for each successful peck. And when the pellets stopped coming, the pigeon stopped pecking. During the second phase of the experiment a week later, the pigeon quickly relearned to peck in the right spot, but this time it only received a pellet for every five correct pecks.

"And then we stopped giving the pellets," I told Shanon, "and for several minutes, the pigeon-pecking increased dramatically. The experiment was supposed to end after five minutes of no pecking, and for a while, we thought this would never happen."

"Did you cheat?" Shanon asked as we waited to cross a street.

"No, but we did threaten the bird with a gruesome death if he didn't stop pecking. 'Don't you dare,' my partners muttered through the glass whenever it looked like it was going to peck. 'Pigeon fried rice?' I suggested. And when the experiment did end, the stupid bird somehow escaped when we tried to transfer it from the cage to an orange juice container we had been given to take it to and from its home cage. After some muttered cursing, my partners were able to sneak up on it from behind and place the container over its head."

"I think the bird got the last laugh," Shanon observed as we turned into the driveway of my apartment building. "See you in a couple of hours."

In my apartment, Jules slept attached to the sofa as I checked my voice mail. One of the boys'-night-out participants had left me a message encouraging me to attend their next get-together the following evening. After leaving him a message stating that I would come if I could, I called my dad, who confirmed that Pat would be coming home on St. Patrick's Day to celebrate her birthday. I called my boss at the London-based corporation to ask if she had reviewed the Reverse Mentoring Program report I had e-mailed her before leaving Guiding Eyes.

"Never mind that," she exclaimed. "How's Jules?"

I launched into a description of our time together.

"I can't wait to meet him when you work with us next month."

My next call was to my boss at the large NGO to ask how things were going there.

"Never mind that!" she exclaimed. "How's Jules? When can I meet him?"

"We might work him there tomorrow."

"I'm not sure where I'll be, but please have the front desk page me when you get here."

Two hours later, Shanon and I began teaching Jules the route between my apartment and the China Café. With Shanon three feet behind me, I worked Jules to the intersection of Calvert Street and Connecticut Avenue, across Calvert Street, and down Connecticut Avenue, where we walked across a long bridge and crossed five quiet streets. We finally arrived at another of those intersections where three streets merged at weird angles.

"Aren't these dogs amazing?" a man with a wheezy voice asked as we began teaching Jules to learn how to handle this new challenge.

"Yes," Shanon said impatiently but kindly. "Dogs can do amazing things."

"Jules, sit," I said under my breath. I shifted from foot to foot.

"God bless them," continued the wheezy voice. "You seem to know a lot about them."

"I train dogs and teach blind people how to work with them."

"God bless you."

Shanon finally succeeded in ending the conversation after several more exchanges. "God bless you both," he called as he walked away.

"He looked like a homeless man," Shanon muttered.

"Oh." I shuffled my feet. "How often does this kind of thing happen when you are training dogs?"

"Once in a while."

We dutifully encouraged Jules to find the correct wheelchair ramp, cross Florida Avenue, walk across a small traffic island, and cross S Street. We then crossed Connecticut Avenue, turned right, and continued down Connecticut for a half block to the China Café.

CHAPTER EIGHT:
ONSTAGE

~

MARCH 15–16, 2005

Over large portions of Chinese fast food, I told Shanon that our encounter with the homeless man had reminded me of how well-meaning strangers would stop my mom and me on the street with such comments as: "Oh, that poor blind boy ... I'm so sorry," or "Isn't it wonderful how well your blind boy can walk?" or "What an amazing mom you are ... God bless you." Social workers trained to work with blind children and their parents would say similar things during home visits and telephone calls. My mom was amazing, but the syrupy ignorance behind these compliments caused her to develop a game to put these remarks in context.

"Five dollars to see Blind Boy tie his shoes!" she would trumpet as she walked with Jenny and me on a Cape Cod beach while the family dogs chased seagulls. "Five dollars to see Blind Boy put on his shirt!" she would proclaim as we walked in the Pleasantville woods while the dogs chased squirrels. "Five dollars to see Blind Boy brush his teeth!" she would declare as we walked the streets of New York City. Jenny and I roared with laughter and eagerly invented more outlandish tasks for me to do for five dollars.

"My goodness," Shanon said.

"The sad thing was that these people had no clue about how amazing my mom was. In addition to brailling materials, fighting for my rights to be educated with sighted kids, and teaching me the skills I would need to live independently, she insisted that I develop my music talents."

"Wow, she sounds incredible."

I told her about how Mom made sure that Jenny and I were exposed to all kinds of music. She taught me the basics of braille music and how to play the piano. When she sensed that I had learned as much as I could from her, she drove me to the Lighthouse for the Blind in New York City every Thursday afternoon for two years. There I gained a greater grasp of braille music through lessons with a church organist who was blind, followed by a ninety-minute piano lesson from a sighted woman with a sappy voice. I continued my piano lessons with an elderly woman with a thick Austrian accent and a no-nonsense attitude who lived near us. While I learned to play more difficult repertoire more skillfully, practicing gradually became a joyless chore. Learning new music was a pain in the neck because I had to learn each measure of each piece first by playing the right-hand part while reading with my left hand. Then I had to play the left-hand part of the same measure while reading with my right hand. Once memorized, I played with both hands without reading the music. I had to repeat this process measure by measure and phrase by phrase until I could play a piece of music from beginning to end.

"Then the chance came for me to learn to play the drums," I said to Shanon, "and I quickly mastered the flams, paradiddles, drags, and drum rolls that form the basis of snare drum technique. I ditched the piano and fell in love after exploring the drum kit of family friends as the adults tried to talk one floor above me."

I absently put my hand on Jules's head as I thought about how my drum practice sessions had given me an emotional outlet as I struggled to adapt to puberty, accept my parents' divorce, and survive the isolation I felt while adjusting to a new school during my freshman year. Better yet, my drum-playing reduced the isolation. In junior high and high school, I jammed with peers, and while I never came close to being a rock star,

I learned about the give-and-take required to be part of a musical group. I also played percussion in school productions of Gilbert and Sullivan operettas and community performances of Broadway musicals.

I described to Shanon how toward the end of my freshman year I had told Mr. V., the high school band director, that I was planning to join the marching band the following year. I argued that I could learn the music by ear and that we could figure out how I could march with the band.

It turned out that learning the music by ear was easy, but performing the simplest maneuvers with the band was impossible. Connecting me by rope with another percussionist caused us both to become entangled as the rest of the band tried to maneuver around us. But Mr. V., instead of giving up, suggested that I stand with him during the half-time maneuvering and that someone could run with me to the percussion section after the completion of the formation, but before they started playing, and then run me back to him as the band started its next marching routine. While I wasn't totally happy with this arrangement, my experience playing with neighborhood kids had taught me that I didn't have to do everything that sighted people could do to be accepted. I was having fun while making a contribution.

"My musical horizons continued to expand," I told Shanon. I talked about how I had sung in Gilbert and Sullivan choruses, choirs, and a Catholic church folk group during high school. I started taking organ lessons during my freshman year of high school, and ended up giving a recital during my sophomore year at Princeton. But while chatting with friends after the recital at a local hotel bar, it dawned on me that I felt no joy from performing as a soloist, just relief that it was over. Two days later, I quit taking organ lessons.

Shanon's cell phone chirped. As she quietly spoke into her phone, I sat back, sipped some ice water, and thought about how laziness had prompted my long-term relationship with composing music. During my junior year of high school, I had persuaded my Bible as Literature teacher to allow me to set six psalms to music instead of writing a term paper. The successful class performances had prompted my organ teacher to persuade the conductor of the Lutheran Church Choir in which I sang to perform three of these psalm settings, and the high school choir had sung one of these settings

96

during my senior year. These successes had prompted me to compose more music, leading to additional performances, and they probably played a pivotal role in my conquest of Princeton's admissions process. I also spent two summers in the Rocky Mountains studying composition at the Aspen Music Festival. Every morning, I worked at a piano in a small wooden cabin, accompanied by bird calls, the rushing waters of a nearby brook, and the random sounds of musicians sharpening their skills. Afternoons and evenings were spent taking classes; working with others to perform music; attending concerts; rafting down the Colorado River; or relaxing with fellow musicians in the dorm, by the river, or at local hang-outs. The skills and confidence I gained recruiting people to play my music and leading rehearsals were critical in my later work assisting groups and organizations in becoming better at what they do.

Shanon apologized as she snapped shut her cell phone.

I laughed. "That's okay; I've been talking too much anyway."

"But how did you have time to do everything?"

I laughed again. "You don't know the half of it." I told her that my senior year in high school was a whirlwind of musical activities: marching band, All-County Band, concert band, high school chorus, Lutheran Church choir, hand-bell choir, organ lessons, trombone lessons, and playing percussion in an opera orchestra.

"But how did you find the time to do all that?" Shanon repeated.

"Well." I paused, dimly aware of the traffic noise seeping through the door. "By that time, I could walk to school and to church using a cane. Mom and I spent lots of time in front of a calendar figuring out who would be responsible for what. It's not that different from how you at Guiding Eyes address the twists and turns while training people to be good dog handlers in all kinds of weather and environments," I continued. "Strong relationships matter; so does sharing a common goal."

"It must have been intense."

"Not really. All that negotiating and running around was fun— sometimes exhilarating."

I described to Shanon how at the beginning of marching band season, Mom had suggested that I find someone to grab my elbow and steer me from behind so I could march with the band. Her solution had worked brilliantly. Mr. V. had found a female volunteer, and I was soon strutting with the band, shouting directions to my fellow drummers over the noise of the drums as she kept me in line with subtle tugs on my elbow and whispered directions in my ear. This solution had worked even better in college since its marching band considered drinking alcohol from concealed flasks as we sat in the stands, and writing sexually charged scripts to be read during halftime shows, to be more important than marching in lockstep to create fancy formations.

"My greatest high school triumph took place during the spring band concert," I told Shanon. The second half had featured two of my compositions and displayed my skills as a percussionist and organist. I had stolen the show and had arrived home to enthusiastic congratulations from the pastor of the Lutheran Church where I sang in the choir. Mom had argued from across the room that I wouldn't have gotten all that applause if I wasn't blind. The pastor had said that it didn't matter, that I had worked hard and deserved the accolades. When Mom had confessed that she wanted to fall through the floor when I got all that applause, the pastor had told her that the night was her triumph as well, and that she should enjoy it.

"I have to go," I had interrupted. "People are waiting to drive me to the post-concert party."

The argument between the pastor and my mom had bounced around in my mind as several of us chatted over large plates of Italian food. *This was a triumph,* I had thought as the conversation swirled around me. As a high school sophomore, I had dreamed of leading the percussion section so that Mr. V. would view us as real musicians instead of noisemaking nuisances. During the fall, I had created and taught the percussion section several new "street beats," those patterns that drummers play to keep the rest of the band marching in time. I had written one of the compositions that had been performed in part to encourage us to sharpen our skills and to bathe in the spotlight instead of hiding behind all of the other instruments. It was challenging, it was fun, and we bonded both as musicians and people.

So yes, that night was a triumph, but several days later a fellow percussionist had told me that he had also been embarrassed by all the applause we had received after playing one of my pieces. "We weren't that good," he had said. "Oh, we were good," I had responded, paused, and then said that I was pretty sure that some of the applause was because I was blind. I reminded him that other soloists had played difficult pieces well but had received far less recognition. "But we were noisier," the percussionist had said as Mr. V. wrapped a music stand with his conductor baton to get our attention.

"But why should it matter?" Shanon asked as we prepared to leave the China Café.

"It shouldn't," I said. "But sometimes people resent it when I get all the attention even though they have worked as hard or harder than I have." We headed to the door. "I also need to know how my skills match up with others in order to compete in a sighted world, and because many sighted people seem to think it's amazing that a blind person can do anything useful, it can be hard to gauge how seriously to internalize a given compliment."

As I worked Jules back to my apartment with Shanon trailing several feet behind me, I was vaguely surprised at how much I had opened up to her; it's remarkable how we will open up to the right person while we're being stretched. After we worked Jules through that three-streets-at-weird-angles intersection, Shanon dropped several feet behind me, and as we walked home in a relaxed silence, I thought about how the he's-amazing-because-he's-blind-and-can-tie-his-shoes syndrome made it difficult to sell myself to hiring managers. I appear at job interviews prepared to talk about my qualifications for a given job, only to be thwarted by a hiring manager's astonishment that a blind person has shown up with a guide dog and without assistance from a sighted person.

"Thanks for coming," an interviewer often says. "How did you get here?"

"I took the subway and walked."

"Amazing."

Interviewers often ask about my professional background or describe the main duties of the job, but while they usually follow the interview script, I sense that my answers are not being absorbed. They sometimes ask how I write reports, and I explain about the software I use that speaks the text that appears on a computer screen. I show them how I can read and write articles, books, and reports using my favorite piece of portable technology.

"Amazing! You can do all that?"

"Of course. I have been doing this for a while."

Interviewers sometimes also ask how I get from place to place, or how I work with a guide dog, or how I read e-mails and navigate the Web, or how I organize my work space, and my responses almost always are greeted with "amazing" or "you're amazing." Thus, my ability to amaze by doing many of the mundane tasks of life independently saturates interviewers' brains, making it impossible for them to absorb how my prior work history could benefit them.

As I worked Jules from the elevator to my apartment, I noticed that my left rear pocket was nearly empty.

"Am I giving Jules too many treats?" I asked, unlocking my door.

"No, you're doing great."

As we reviewed the day's events, Jules shook himself, drank some water, rolled on his back, and began pawing under the sofa.

"Would it be all right if I hung out with a few friends at a local restaurant?" I asked, remembering the voice mail about the boys'-night-out get-together.

Jules continued pawing under the sofa. "Do you expect me to give you that piece of kibble, you brat?" Shanon asked. She stuck her hand under the sofa to retrieve the morsel. "Take it," she said with a smile in her voice. "What was that?" Shanon asked me as he devoured his last treat of the day.

I repeated the question.

"I wouldn't if I were you," she said. "It's been a long day, and you both need to relax."

I sighed as she collected her things. "I thought that's what you'd say. But I know you're right." And she was right, I reflected as we said our good-byes. My top priority was to build that bond with Jules, and putting too much pressure might destroy what we were creating. While I was vaguely disappointed that I wouldn't be hanging out with the guys, I knew my friends would understand, as some had guide dogs. *And there will be plenty of chances to hang out,* I thought as I settled down for a quiet evening and a good night's sleep.

The next morning, Shanon, Jules, and I met in the lobby of my apartment building. Again, his harness was on, his tail was wagging, and my left rear pocket was full of treats. As we retraced our steps to the China Café, I became more conscious of the little missteps we were making. Just as we were ready to cross Calvert Street, Shanon warned me that my body was facing a bit too much toward Connecticut Avenue. "And you might also want to tell Jules to pay attention to you instead of that pigeon on the other side of the street," she added.

After making sure that my body and feet were facing Calvert Street, I distracted Jules from the pigeon by calling his name sharply and giving him a treat.

"Much better," Shanon said.

While we waited for the parallel traffic to start moving, I told her of a harrowing crossing of Calvert Street that Gifford and I had made during our early days together. "I thought we were crossing Calvert Street, but I knew I was in trouble when I heard traffic zooming all around us. I've crossed thousands of city streets in all kinds of weather, hollering at drivers who cut in front of me that they were assholes and that I could drive better than they could. I learned to trust the judgments of my dogs. But crossing when I knew the light was against me was terrifying. 'Hurry up!' I screamed at Gifford, and we somehow made it across unscathed."

"My goodness."

"Jules, forward! Good boy!" I gushed when we reached the up-curb, where I gave him a treat.

Shortly afterward, I grazed a pole with my right arm. "No!" I said, giving him a leash correction. "Sit!" I ordered, tapping the pole. I walked backward several feet and ordered him "forward," and I felt him veer to the left. "Good boy! Take that treat!"

As we continued walking, I found myself wondering why Jules was slowing down. Was the sidewalk too crowded? Was he focused on something else? Was he becoming too stressed? And what should I do about this? Most often, it was best to trust him to do the right thing, but it might be better to use my voice to get his attention or to give him a leash correction. "Lots of people on the sidewalk," Shanon called. When he slowed down a second time, she told me that he was glaring at another pigeon. "Come on, Jules!" I snapped, and sensed his head move toward me and his pace quicken. "Good boy!"

Later, I wondered why he was veering me nearer to the parallel traffic than I thought he should. Was he avoiding an obstacle? Was he trying to scent-sniff or flirt with another human? Did he need to park? Was he overtired? Again, it was usually best to trust him to do the right thing, but it might be better to command him to do something different or to give him a leash correction or allow him to park. "Jules is trying to lead you around a car parked on the sidewalk," Shanon explained.

"You would think that I could do a better job figuring out why Jules is doing what he's doing after working with four dogs," I said as we relaxed in the sun outside of the China Café.

"This is one of the reasons why we don't mail you your fully trained dog in a box along with a how-to manual."

"Yes, but—"

"And you don't have to guess right every time. Jules will survive an occasional unjust harsh word or leash correction if the bond between you is strong enough."

"Are we bonding, Jules?" I leaned down to hug him, and he shook himself and wagged his tail.

Back at the apartment, I called Dad, who confirmed that Pat would be coming home the following afternoon to celebrate her birthday. He told me that the house was being made ready for her return. I heard their toy poodle yapping in the background. "Even Happy knows something exciting is about to happen," he said with a chuckle.

The afternoon trip to the large NGO began with me working Jules the short distance between my apartment and the Woodley Park Metro station. With Shanon three feet behind us, we rode down two escalators, the second of which is one of the longest in the Metro system. As we

102

whirred downward, I remembered how Nan the chocolate Lab would hop on an escalator and then turn her body to prevent anyone from passing us.

"Excuse me, can I get by?" fellow riders would whine.

"Come on, Nan!" I turned her eighty-pound body so she was parallel to me.

"Thank you." A pedestrian would try to pass us only to be thwarted by Nan who again had turned to barricade the passage. "Oh, never mind."

Once at the bottom of the second escalator, I encouraged Jules to find the place where I would feed my fare card through a slot prompting a gate to open and allowing us to walk through. He led me forward at his usual brisk pace, but I soon realized that I couldn't give him clear directions because I had forgotten how to get there without relying on Gifford's ability to find any fare gate within the Metro system. And I couldn't hear the sounds of people swiping their cards and the whirring of opening and closing gates that I used as cues.

"Shanon, help," I whispered over my shoulder.

"Tell Jules to turn right as soon as he can, and the gates will be straight ahead," her voice echoed back.

"Thanks," I said over my shoulder. "Good boy!" I told Jules when we arrived. "Take that treat!"

Once through the gate, we headed down a short escalator and walked about one hundred feet on the platform. We turned left to face the tracks on which the train would arrive. As we waited, I told Shanon about how Heidi and Nan would drag me onto a New York City subway car as soon as the door rattled open, without waiting for passengers to get off. "Can't you wait until we get off?" some would grouse while brushing past us onto the platform. "Don't worry," others would say from the safety of their seats, "your dog is a true New Yorker."

"Some dogs are more assertive than others," Shanon pointed out.

"True," I said, as my next two dogs were more likely to wait for passengers to get off before we boarded. "Or perhaps Dunbar and Gifford were less stressed in the DC Metro, which is more laid back than the noisier, smellier, and more crowded New York City subways."

"Possibly."

"Or maybe," I mused as I heard the train approaching from my left, "they were calmer because I have mellowed with age."

Jules stood calmly by my side as the incoming rumble increased to a roar. When the train screeched to a stop, I ordered him, "Forward! To the door!" As we headed down the platform, I heard the soft whir of the opening doors. We gradually slowed down and stopped as we approached the spot where the whirring noise seemed to come from. "He's waiting for passengers to get off," Shanon said quietly. After several seconds, she told me that the coast was clear. "Good boy! Forward! To the door," I repeated, and he turned left leading me inside.

"Nice," Shanon said. The doors closed. "There are two seats across from us."

I gave Jules a treat and followed her to the seats, where I told him to sit, making sure his head was facing forward. Like Gifford, he preferred to lie down, so I pushed him under the seat so that other passengers would be less likely to step on his paws.

As the train started moving, I told Shanon that I could usually find an empty seat when a car was not too crowded, and that I was happy to stand if none seemed available. But many passengers would offer me their seats. "It's okay," I would say impatiently as a New York City subway car pulled out of the station. "I'm fine; please stay there." I had no other disabilities, and it seemed unfair to take the seat of someone who sounded old enough to be a grandparent or tired after a long day. While many accepted, others would get up anyway, often without telling me.

"DuPont Circle," the conductor's voice blared over the PA system as the train slowed down and stopped.

"You might want to tell Jules to sit so that he won't be stepped on," Shanon suggested.

He ignored my first "sit" command. I tried again, using a leash correction. He sat, but tried to lie down. "No! Sit, you lazy Labrador!" I hissed, giving him another leash correction. He obeyed, but collapsed to the floor with a thud when the doors closed.

"Next stop, Farragut North!"

"That's our stop," I said, relieved that I wouldn't have to fight the keep-Jules-at-sit battle again.

"However, when I moved to DC," I continued, "it seemed less important to reject the offer of seats. I still refused if the passenger seemed older, but the trains were usually less crowded. And I'm getting older too."

We left the train at Farragut North, rode up an escalator, went through a fare gate, and rode up another longer escalator to the street. As I began working Jules to the NGO, I confessed that a street we were about to cross made me edgy.

"We'll take a look at it when we get there," Shanon said, and as we approached the intersection, she observed that the traffic patterns looked nasty. "Tell me when you think it's safe to cross."

"Now?" I asked when I thought the parallel traffic had started moving.

"Yes, go ahead."

"Jules, forward!" I commanded in as confident a voice as I could muster, and he briskly guided me to a traffic island in the middle of the street, across the traffic island, and across the rest of the street. "Good boy," I said, tapping the up-curb with my foot. "Take that treat!"

"Very nice," Shanon said.

"And then there's the small matter that a car grazed the upper part of my right arm last July," I said as we continued to walk to the NGO. "Gifford and I were hurrying to a meeting, and when I arrived at that intersection, I was sure the parallel traffic had just started moving. So we started crossing the street, but just after we stepped off of that traffic island, this car whizzed by and clipped my right arm just above the elbow."

"How did Gifford react?"

"It didn't faze him a bit. We continued to the NGO, where I took part in a ninety-minute meeting while the back of my arm stung and drops of blood fell on the carpet."

"You're crazy."

"My boss said the same thing. She asked me after the meeting what had happened to my arm, and when I told her, she gasped theatrically and shouted the news to anyone within earshot. I had stammered that I was late, it didn't hurt too much, and I didn't want to interrupt the flow of the meeting. Clucking in disbelief, she had taken me to a nurse in the basement of the building who disinfected and bandaged the scratches, gave me some pain pills, and sent me home in a cab.

"You are aware that the traffic patterns after the traffic island are controlled by a different set of lights?" Shanon asked as we walked across a quieter street.

"I sort of figured that out afterwards," I said sheepishly, for I knew that I was lucky that Gifford or I had not been more seriously injured. I also knew that skirmishes with cars had derailed other person-dog teams. Sometimes, the handler loses faith in his or her dog. Sometimes, dogs can become skittish in traffic or just refuse to work. But Gifford's enthusiasm, confidence, and competence never waned, thus strengthening our trust in each other.

CHAPTER NINE:
MAKING CONNECTIONS

MARCH 16, 2005

S hanon and I sat on a couch in the lobby of the NGO with Jules under my feet as a security guard tried to locate my boss.

"This place is crazy," she whispered as employees and visitors hurried about, their voices echoing throughout the lobby.

"What do you mean?" Jules rolled on his back, pawed the couch, and snorted.

"The ceilings are really high, and there are lots of paintings everywhere."

The commotion continued to swirl around us. "I'm wearing the wrong clothes," Shanon exclaimed.

"What are you wearing?" I asked, aware of the organization's button-down ways.

"Jeans and a sweatshirt."

"Don't worry; my boss won't care. I should be wearing a suit instead of a short-sleeved shirt and khaki slacks."

"I could never work here," she said after another pause. "Too many people, too much pretense. Give me the freedom of the outdoors."

I told her that I understood, and that many employees found the place confining as well. "It's rather sad," I explained, "because people come to work here from all over the world. Most of them have advanced degrees from the best schools, and they get paid very well. But the bureaucracy discourages them from thinking outside of the box."

"Excuse me, sir," the security guard interrupted, "but I cannot find your boss."

"Thanks for your efforts," I said with a sigh as we got up to leave.

We stopped at a Quiznos on the way home to relax over sandwiches, chips, and sodas. While Jules slept under the table, I told Shanon that Guiding Eyes could teach other organizations a thing or two.

"Like what?"

I explained that both the NGO and Guiding Eyes have clear missions, but that Guiding Eyes staff seems much happier even though the NGO pays much better.

"I don't do this work for the money."

"Of course you don't. So what keeps you going?"

Shanon crunched a potato chip. "I like the people I work with. Seeing blind people succeed with their dogs is rewarding. And my bosses give me freedom to decide how best to get the job done."

"So they're not breathing down your neck to be sure that you are doing your job?"

"No."

"There's the difference. The NGO staff that I have worked with chafes at the constraints their bosses place upon them. Over time, these constraints cause employees to think more about playing the system instead of working to fulfill the organization's mission."

As we rose to continue our journey back to my apartment, I observed that many things had changed for the better at Guiding Eyes over the years. Staff had learned to adjust the training to the needs of each student. The atmosphere was mellower, the living conditions were more comfortable, and the food was better. "But," I continued, "one thing that hasn't changed is the high expectations placed on the students. It's refreshing to go to a condescension-free zone."

"We meet many interesting blind people from all walks of life, so we sort of learn to expect great things from them," Shanon said as we waited for the train to take us back to Woodley Park.

"There's more to it than that. Remember my mom's reaction to those social workers, or the general contempt blind people have towards VR counselors? Each of these well-meaning helpers has an equal chance to meet many interesting blind people throughout their careers, yet we still find many of them to be condescending."

I asked her about her career path at Guiding Eyes. Like Pam, she had started as an instructor's assistant and had eventually been assigned to a team of more experienced instructors to learn the skills she would need to work with both dogs and people with visual impairments.

"And one of the things you learned was how not to treat blind adults as children?"

"I guess," she said as the train approached from right to left.

After getting onto the train and settling into two seats, I told Shanon that I had heard that a part of the instructor training included spending ten days in class with other visually impaired students while wearing a blindfold. She said that she and her colleagues had found this part of the program very valuable. "Learning to eat without making a mess was the hardest," she continued. "During the first breakfast, I tried to pour juice into a glass without first checking to be sure that it was right side up. A colleague knocked over a full glass of milk during her first meal."

Shanon spoke of running headfirst into objects, sitting on the floor instead of the bed, and searching for lost items. She talked about her surprise at how stressed she had become during the last three days under blindfold and the bond she felt toward the dog that she had been matched with. She also described how her fellow visually impaired students had given her emotional support while teaching her some of the techniques we use to make our lives a little easier: beginning the search for a lost object close to ourselves and then gradually extending the search outward in ever-widening circles until we find it; learning about surroundings by listening to how footsteps and other sounds bounce off objects; and identifying the location of a chair with a hand before trying to sit down.

"So what did you learn?" I asked as we rode up the long Woodley Park escalator.

She said that the briefing she received prior to wearing the blindfold alerted her to the challenges she might face, but experiencing life as a blind person training to work with a guide dog made it real.

"I understand better the challenges that people with visual impairments face," she continued, "as well as the tools they use to survive." She also talked about how she had found it difficult to stay awake during the daily lectures. "I now make an effort to walk around while I'm speaking so that students don't hear my voice coming from the same place. I try to make the experience more of a conversation than a lecture by asking questions, cracking jokes, and encouraging more experienced guide dog users to share their stories."

So Shanon learned the craft of guide dog training through working with more seasoned instructors, I mused as we made the short walk to my apartment building. She had also learned about the challenges that her visually impaired "customers" face and some of the strategies used to address them. She had become motivated to improve her presentation skills. And all this without large training budgets and legions of bureaucrats so common in larger organizations.

"And there's at least one more thing other organizations might learn from Guiding Eyes," I said as we entered my apartment. I sensed that she was ready to leave, but I was on too much of a roll. "Many employers are trying to assist older and younger workers in communicating better with each other. This is especially a problem when young managers are supervising workers old enough to be their parents or grandparents. But Guiding Eyes instructors in their twenties and thirties often teach visually impaired people in their sixties and seventies to be effective guide dog handlers."

"The two situations aren't quite the same," Shanon said as she sat on the couch to which Jules was tied.

"You're right. Teaching someone to do something new is only part of a supervisor's job, but still—"

Jules shook himself as I put my backpack on the closet shelf and sat on my bed facing her.

"Many of these students are coming back for their third, fourth, or fifth dog, so I often learn a lot from these experienced dog handlers."

"That makes sense."

"No! No! No!" Shanon said in her kind, firm dog-handler voice.

"What is he doing?"

"He's pawing me to get my attention! You brat!" She laughed as she walked away from his paw toward the apartment door. Laughing, I followed her. Jules shook himself as we said our good-byes.

Graham later expanded upon Shanon's interrupted musings.

"I remember that when I first started I was so grateful to work with the returning students," he told me. "They patiently showed me methods that worked and were safe. They never made me feel inexperienced or stupid, and I vowed to keep that philosophy as I gained experience." He went on to say that young instructors are encouraged to take on an I-will-work-with-you attitude rather than a this-is-the-only-way mind-set. "It is when they threaten to adopt the latter philosophy that they experience problems," he concluded.

Becky, the manager of Consumer Outreach, added another piece to the puzzle.

"It is important that every student work his or her dog long enough while here so that they can begin to adjust to each other," she said, "but a few of our older students sometimes have trouble completing some of the longer routes. If instructors notice that a student is struggling, they might suggest that they stop somewhere for a cup of coffee so that the student can relax for a few minutes before finishing the route."

As I flopped down on my bed and turned the radio onto WTOP, DC's all-news radio station, I thought about the things that made Guiding Eyes such a special organization: flexibility, patience, a customer focus, trust, modeling effective behavior, building on strengths, and "selling" a mission. These components are powerful tools for anyone engaged in leading others. Those organizations that don't value these tools because they are too "soft and squishy" are likely to lose both customers and money. Why? Because research shows that top employees leave when they don't understand what's expected of them, think that their talents don't match job tasks, believe they are not getting what they need to do their job effectively, sense that their bosses don't appreciate their good work, or haven't developed friendships with others in the organization. Front-line managers are in the best position to meet these needs and therefore play a pivotal role in determining how many top performers stay or leave.

All organizations claim that they want their staff to be the best that they can be. Yet executives of too many organizations underestimate the importance of front-line managers. They often promote their best performers into management without trying to figure out if they have what it takes to do the job. They encourage managers to "fix" employee limitations instead of building on their strengths. These actions drive away top performers while breeding cynicism and apathy among those who remain.

People with disabilities, along with people from other minority groups, usually suffer more from inept bosses because we often have unique needs that must be met for us to be successful. In order to be productive, I must be certain that the software that "speaks" the text on a computer screen works well within an employer's computer network. I must learn how to travel to the office from home and how to find my desk, as well as the bathroom, kitchen, meeting rooms, elevator, and other key locations within and around the office. And I must begin to develop relationships with my colleagues, many of whom have never met a blind person before. While I am responsible for laying the foundation for my success, inept supervisors have made this transition more difficult by failing to connect me with the resources I need and conveying little confidence in my abilities to my colleagues.

Jules sighed contentedly as I remembered my positive experiences with bosses. My first job after receiving my MSW was to manage a nationwide project aimed at linking twelve universities with local employers to develop strategies that would improve employment opportunities for college students with disabilities. When Nan the chocolate Lab and I arrived for our first day of work, an administrative assistant gave us a brief tour, introducing us to her colleagues along the way. She then ushered us to my office, where I found project-related materials in braille on my desk. I attached Nan to a chair and began reading.

"Hi," a cheerful voice had called an hour later from outside my office door. "I'm Lana, the project director."

I put the materials on my desk and stood up quickly as she walked into my office. "Hi," I said, reaching out my hand toward her.

We shook hands. "Hi, Nan," she said.

"It's not a good idea to talk to her when she's in harness," I muttered.

"I know." Lana chuckled. "But she licked my hand."

"She likes to break rules, like her human," I said. We both laughed, and Lana said that she had come by to answer any questions that I might have. I told her that the project's scope seemed overwhelming.

"Yes, it is complicated, and we should have started working on it two months ago. But we wanted to find the right person, and we think that you are that person."

For the next several minutes, we discussed project details: phone calls to make, letters to write, meetings to organize, and records to keep. "Nan, behave," she had ordered as she walked out of the office, leaving behind a can-do spirit.

During the next three years, I conducted meetings so that disabled students, college administrators, and corporate staff could develop action plans; coached participants in how best to work together; developed training programs; and presented project findings at several conferences. This was a major change from my prior customer service work, and I wasn't certain that I was ready for the challenges. I often felt as if I was juggling twelve balls in the air as we assisted those twelve university-employer partnerships in forming and growing. The work was exhilarating and occasionally overwhelming, for I never quite knew what I would be doing from one day to the next.

As the project developed, I came to look forward to wandering into Lana's office at the end of the day—when one of us wasn't traveling—to discuss project details, an idea, office politics, or life in general. She would focus me on project goals whenever I got too caught up in details. She assisted me in translating an idea into a program or workshop. And she empathized when I griped about how no one in the organization seemed to understand what the project was about ("We could do this work better from my garage," she would often say) while working with me to find ways to connect with my colleagues. When we worked together on the road, she allowed me to take charge of meetings and workshops, providing suggestions during breaks and occasionally alerting me to visual but soundless cues from the back of the room. "Peter," she would say, "someone has his hand in the air," or "someone was just about to say something," but allowing me to decide how to respond. By project's end, I had developed a whole new set of skills and a confidence in my abilities.

For the next three years, Dunbar and I traveled throughout New York State to assist public school administrators, software vendors, and parents in working together to improve the way technology was made available to students with disabilities. With him at my side, I also conducted workshops to improve customer service skills of New York City taxi drivers, led discussions to encourage people to work toward common goals despite racial and gender differences, and assisted in the creation of a virtual community of people interested in improving employment opportunities for people with visual impairments. By the time we arrived in Washington, DC, for my new job at that small NGO, I had developed a professional swagger.

"I reviewed the process that you use to organize and lead dialogues among pro-choice and pro-life activists," I announced to my new boss, Mary, during the morning of my fifth day on the job, "and I find it *way* too confining." I went on to describe my successes leading conversations between groups that didn't trust each other, as well as the similarities and differences I saw between our approaches. Mary argued that the lack of trust among abortion activists was higher than the trust among the groups I had been working with. "Many pro-life activists compare abortion to the Holocaust," she reminded me, "and a small minority has bombed clinics where abortions take place and murdered doctors who perform abortions. And many pro-choice activists accuse pro-lifers of hating women and of secretly supporting the bombings and murders."

"You're probably right," I conceded as Dunbar lay down with a grunt, "but do you really believe that requiring dialogue participants to sign a piece of paper listing required behaviors affects the way they talk to each other?"

114

"Many activists won't participate without witnessing those on the other side signing that piece of paper," Mary countered. She went on to describe how she and a partner developed and put together the components of the dialogue over three years of trial and error.

"But I believe that if you rely too much on structure, participants begin to feel like children and are less likely to say what they really believe," I told her. "This breeds resentment and prevents relationships from growing."

"But you have to remember that the lack of trust is much higher among these activists than the trust among the groups you have worked with."

"But—"

"And besides, the process works. We have activists from all over the country talking instead of hurling insults at each other, and some groups are working together toward goals on which they can agree: preventing teen pregnancy, promoting adoption, and advocating for better programs to support women and children."

"True. But I'm sure the folks you find to lead these dialogue groups modify your approach as they go along."

"I guess that's possible." She paused. "But I'm in constant touch with both dialogue leaders and participants, and they depend on the approach."

"But—"

"You need to lose that New York City attitude!"

That brought me up short, for I knew I was pushing too hard. After all, I had moved to DC to take this job in part because I wanted to learn more about assisting people in having respectful conversations about difficult topics. Mary had spent a summer Saturday morning to help me find an apartment within walking distance from the office and allowed me to take a few personal days so I could become familiar with the neighborhood.

"You're right," I told Mary a few minutes later, "and I'm sorry. You know far more about this than I do, and I will do my best to be less arrogant."

She accepted my apology and allowed me to start a New York City dialogue group a week later. I also spent many weeks in Glendale, Arizona, assisting the group there in organizing a dialogue among community leaders, parents, and high school students to develop strategies to prevent teen pregnancy. This work resulted in an invitation to a reception at the White House where Hillary Clinton spoke about the importance of inspiring and supporting young adults to develop goals and make wise decisions. Afterward, Mary, Dunbar, and I walked to another part of the White House complex to meet her niece who was serving as a White House intern. As soon as we entered the office, Dunbar started sniffing the carpet.

"Why is he sniffing?" I wondered aloud.

"Buddy just left," the intern explained.

"Buddy? The Clinton family dog?"

"Yes. The Secret Service brings him here all the time."

Our work bringing pro-life and pro-choice activists together was so countercultural that no private foundations would fund it. A representative of one left-leaning foundation told us that they would be happy to give us money if we could co-opt pro-lifers to join them in their efforts, and none of the right-leaning foundations we contacted bothered to respond.

As our work together wound down, I told Mary how much I enjoyed working with her. "Remember how Dunbar would drag me to your desk at the beginning of each day?"

"He came by to say good morning."

"Hardly. He wanted a piece of your muffin."

"Why are you so cynical? Dunbar loved me."

"Oh, c'mon. This is Dunbar, the one who devoured a bowl of cereal that was on your kitchen table when I spent the night at your house."

"But he loves me for me as well."

I smiled. "Of course he does."

"And I will never forget how stunned you were when we arrived at the gate at the airport in Baltimore for our flight to Chicago," I told her. "We couldn't walk together because you needed me to help carry a piece of luggage. So I held onto Dunbar's harness in my left hand while carrying the suitcase in my right hand with a battered briefcase on my back. And you were walking several feet behind me giving me directions."

Mary laughed. "I was unprepared for how fast we would walk and how Dunbar's take-charge attitude would cause crowds to scatter."

I thanked her for standing her ground when my arrogance got the better of me and for her suggestions and gentle encouragement when I called to complain about the Arizona heat or the inability of some to accept that I could be both useful and blind. I thanked her for her willingness to allow me to try new things even though a couple of our "customers" expressed some concerns. And I told her how much I appreciated her modeling the behavior she wanted instead of talking at me about what she expected.

Flexibility, patience, a customer focus, trust, modeling effective behavior, building on strengths, and "selling" a mission are indeed powerful tools for someone engaged in leading others to accomplish great things. Over time, the bad bosses brought out the worst in me, resulting in too many snippy exchanges with customers and an unquenchable wish to snicker with my colleagues about the stupidities of the system. The better bosses brought out the best in me, resulting in higher quality work and a willingness either to tolerate or help change things for the better.

And customers can sense the difference, I thought as I put two handfuls of kibble in Jules's food bowl. "We never would have met if I didn't value what Guiding Eyes has to offer," I told him. I put the bowl on the ground and ruffled his fur. "And that would have been so sad."

Jules thumped his tail against the wall and began eating.

Gifford during retirement

Gifford during retirement

Jules as a puppy

Jules as a puppy

PART III:

SAYING GOOD-BYES

CHAPTER TEN:
A DUNBAR FACTOR
~
MARCH 17–20, 2005

The next morning, I worked Jules again to Popeyes, with Shanon dropping back from her usual three feet behind us to half a city block. She would be returning to Guiding Eyes the following afternoon, and Jules and I needed to begin to get used to working together alone. All went well until we reached that three-streets-at-weird-angles intersection.

"Jules, forward!" I said. He moved ahead and started veering to the right instead of straight across the street.

"Jules, what *are* you doing?"

"He's trying to cross two streets at the same time," Shanon called.

All of my prior dogs had tried to cut corners as they became familiar with the routes we walked. "I know where we're going," they seemed to be saying, "so why cross the first street to the curb, turn to face the other street of the intersection, wait for a while, and then cross the second street?" Since this was usually a quiet intersection and I didn't hear any traffic noises, I didn't feel in any danger. On the other hand, mind-reading is not part of a guide dog's responsibilities.

"No!" I told Jules firmly. I gave him a leash correction and tried to get him back on course.

"Let him finish doing the wrong thing," Shanon said as she caught up with us, "and we'll make him do it right."

When we reached the curb, I gave him another leash correction. "Jules, heel!" I commanded. I grabbed Shanon's left elbow so she could lead us back to where the trouble began.

"Let's try this again." We faced the intersection. "Okay ... Jules, forward! Good boy!" I gushed as we headed straight across the street. "Good boy!" I said again as we stepped onto the sidewalk. "Take that treat!"

He devoured another treat as we arrived at the Popeyes counter.

"Five pieces spicy dark meat and large fries?" a woman with a Spanish accent asked from behind the counter.

"Yes, thanks."

"Is that your new dog?"

"Yes. His name is Jules."

"Nice dog." I gave her a twenty-dollar bill that I had folded three times to distinguish it from one-, five-, and ten-dollar bills.

"Here are the singles," she said. I put them unfolded into my wallet. "And here's the ten." I thanked her as I folded it twice before putting it away. She handed me my bag of food, which I stuffed into my backpack.

"I assume you only fold five-dollar bills once?" Shanon asked as we left the restaurant.

"That's right," I said, imagining myself tearing into that wonderfully greasy food. "Jules, forward!"

I was eager to get home, but he began slowing down. I didn't want to pressure him to speed up because he needed time and space to find a path through the noisy crowds around us. I also knew that it took time for new dogs to gain the endurance to tackle long, complex routes. I hoped that he would pick up the pace when the crowds thinned out, but he continued to slow down. I could feel his head turning away from the street.

"He's looking at the dogs and children in a park we're walking by," Shanon called. "He wants to go there instead of back to your apartment."

"Come on, Jules, I'm hungry," I told him, but he continued to slow down.

"Oh come on, you lazy Labrador, you can do better than that!" I growled, but he continued to dawdle, finally stopping in the middle of the sidewalk.

"You're being too nice," Shanon called.

"Jules, *forward!*" I barked, reinforcing the command with a leash correction. He moved out lethargically, but after several additional leash corrections and encouraging words, we were back to our normal pace. "Good boy, Jules!" I said cheerfully. "I'll see you in a couple of hours," I told Shanon outside my apartment door. I tied Jules to the sofa and devoured my Popeyes meal.

The afternoon route involved taking the Metro for one stop and returning home on foot, passing the China Café along the way. Much to our delight, Jules guided me flawlessly through the rush-hour crowds and across busy intersections without allowing pigeons, squealing children, and barking dogs to distract him.

"I'm leaving," Shanon quipped as we rode the elevator to the sixth floor. "You guys don't need me anymore."

Perhaps not, I thought as I prepared for an afternoon nap. I also knew though, from working with my prior dogs, that there would be days when one or both of us would be distracted and fail to react to the other's subtle signals. But I was confident that these bad days would become nothing but memories as we continued to work together.

The warbling phone jarred me awake.

"Hello?"

"Hi, this is your dad."

"Hi, how's Pat?" I felt guilty for not calling to welcome her home and to wish her a happy birthday.

"She's dead."

"She's *what?*"

"She's dead. She died about an hour ago."

"But I thought she was well enough to come home."

Hiding his feelings behind a wall of grumpiness, Dad described how she had been carried upstairs to her bedroom, where the oxygen tanks and other medical equipment had been put in place. He described how Happy the toy poodle had bounded upstairs and licked every inch of her face. "And then she stopped breathing, and the medics couldn't revive her."

"I don't know what to say," I stammered. "I mean, I'm sorry. I'll miss her and all that, but I didn't know that she might die soon." The phone was silent in my hand. "When's the funeral?"

"I don't know. I'll call you when I know more."

I told him that I would call my sister, Jenny, with the news.

"Thank you." This was the first time I could remember him sharing any emotionally laden news, and he seemed grateful not to have to do it again. I asked if he was all right.

"Yes. Pamela, Scott, and Diane are here." Pamela had been Pat's live-in housekeeper for nearly forty years, and Pat had befriended Scott, Diane, and their son, Joey, when they moved next door ten years earlier.

How could Pat be dead? I wondered numbly as I left the news on Jenny's voice mail. *And how come nobody told me she was in danger of dying?*

You shouldn't be so surprised, my social-work side chided as I went through the motions of filling Jules's food and water bowls. *Keeping and sharing secrets was a big part of how the three of you operated.* It was common for both of them to tell me something and then say, "Now whatever you do, please don't tell your dad," or "Don't tell Pat; she won't understand."

Then I recalled a conversation between Pat and me on Christmas night of last year. Gifford and I were getting ready for bed when she asked me to come into her room.

"Peter," she had begun, "I want you to know that I do not have lung cancer."

"You what?"

"You might have heard that I have lung cancer, but it isn't true."

"Okay," I had said, not knowing what to think. She had smoked at least two packs of cigarettes a day for at least thirty years, but this was the first time I had heard the words "lung cancer" in connection with her health.

"You must believe me," she had insisted. "I do not have lung cancer."

"I believe you." We had hugged. "Thanks for the wonderful Christmas dinner."

"It was nothing. Good night, dahling."

I wondered how I would handle traveling alone with Jules to Trenton for the funeral. We were in his park area, and the raucous sounds of a St. Patrick's Day celebration floated to us from an Irish pub across the street. I knew that Guiding Eyes usually encouraged recently graduated teams not to travel to new places for several weeks so that they could establish a predictable routine. On the other hand, the school had given its blessing for Gifford and me to visit New York City a week after we were on our own. We had taken the Metro to Union Station and had ridden the Amtrak train to New York City's Penn Station, where an Amtrak employee had assisted us to the Seventh Avenue and Thirty-fourth Street exit. Once outside, I had picked up his harness handle and urged him "forward," and off we went, weaving through the crowded New York City sidewalks and across eight busy intersections until we had arrived at a large office building where we had charged through a revolving door. "Good boy!" I had said a bit too loudly because I was so excited that he, like me, thrived on the high energy of the city.

"Excuse me, sir," came the more dignified voice of what I presumed to be a security guard. "Can I help you?"

I had explained that I was scheduled to take part in a job interview, and he had steered us to the elevator.

"Thank you for coming," the interviewer had said a few minutes later as she ushered us into her office. "How was the trip?"

"No problem." Gifford had grunted as he lay down under my chair.

"That dog is so well-behaved. How long have you had it? Two years?"

"Actually, we've been together for three weeks."

"Those dogs are really amazing."

The interviewer, though impressed with Gifford's professionalism, had hired someone else.

"Come on, get busy," I coaxed, but Jules, perhaps picking up on my preoccupation, stood still sniffing the cool air, with his head pointing to the celebration across the street.

As we rode the elevator down to the lobby to begin our last day with Shanon, I was still trying to wrap my head around the idea that Pat was dead and that no one had told me about the seriousness of her illness during the past month. But I had become pretty adept had compartmentalizing my feelings. While growing up, Mom had told Jenny and me that our tasks had to get done no matter how we felt. In fifth grade, I had played a piano piece particularly well during a lesson thirty minutes after learning that a beloved teacher had died suddenly. I had learned to control my nervousness prior to a performance, job interview, or presentation. And I wanted all the support I could get from Shanon.

For the morning trip, I worked Jules to the Manhattan Market, where I had shopped every Saturday morning for six years. "The route's pretty easy," I explained as we headed out of my apartment building. "Once I cross Connecticut Avenue, I turn right and continue down Connecticut until I hear the bark of a large dog named Bruiser. Then I have to persuade Jules that we want to visit the store just beyond the barking dog."

But I began having second thoughts as we crossed Connecticut Avenue with Shanon trailing us. Would Bruiser play his role properly? He had always barked ferociously whenever he saw us coming, and Gifford would bark right back. At first, I tried to discourage the barking with the usual combination of a firm "no" and leash correction, but when these efforts failed, I tried a new approach adapted from my dad's technique to prepare our first family dog, Suzie, for her confrontations with a neighborhood border collie named Tammy. Almost every morning, he would goad her into indignant whining by asking, "Where's Tammy?" in a falsely innocent voice as he drove Jenny and me to the bus stop. She would let loose with a volley of vicious barks whenever Tammy started chasing our car. "Good girl! You tell her!" we would shout from the backseat as Dad chuckled from behind the wheel.

"Where's that stupid vicious dog?" I began asking Gifford in a falsely innocent voice after we had crossed Connecticut Avenue and started heading for the store. "Good boy!" I had encouraged as he picked up his pace.

"Woof! Woof! *Woof!*" Bruiser had challenged as we approached his territory.

"Woof! Woof! *Woof!*" Gifford shouted back.

"Now, Gifford," I would say in the calmest voice I could muster, "you really don't want to fight with that stupid dog. You're way too smart for that."

The intensity of the barking increased as we drew even with Bruiser, but Gifford would slow down only slightly as we passed by before turning into the grocery store. "Good boy, Gifford!" I would say as the door muted Bruiser's racket.

So will Bruiser, the audible landmark, bark when he sees me coming with another dog? I worried as I sped closer and closer to the store. Cars, trucks, and bicycles whizzed by. A Metro train rumbled past underneath my feet. But no barking.

"Have we passed the store?" I asked over my shoulder.

"Not yet, but you're getting close."

"Woof, woof," the canine landmark lazily called a few seconds later.

"Good boy," I told Jules, for he only briefly turned his head toward the noise. We eased past Bruiser into the store.

"Hey, Pete," said Rick, a former Vietnam veteran who ran the store. Every Saturday morning for the past six years, he had retrieved the groceries I needed. "How're things going with Jules?"

"Fine. Unlike Gifford, he ignored Bruiser."

"It was strange how two laid-back male black Labs could dislike each other so much."

"It was weird that Bruiser was the only dog that brought out Gifford's aggression."

"But they were both large male dogs," Shanon pointed out from the door.

After I introduced Rick to Shanon, he asked me what I needed.

"A quart of skimmed milk, a quart of orange juice, and six green bananas—"

"I'll do that," Shanon interrupted.

"Don't worry. We do this all the time," Rick protested.

"You stay there; I'll help Peter get what he needs."

So while Rick stayed up front, Shanon, Jules, and I walked through the cramped aisles to pick up not just the milk, orange juice, and bananas, but also raisin bran, hot pockets, Spicy Nacho Doritos, Ivory dishwashing soap, toilet paper, pita bread, butter, and Ben and Jerry's New York Super Fudge Chunk ice cream.

"Is that all you need?" she asked as we approached the cash register.

"Yes, I'm fine," I assured her. "Don't forget that I am a confirmed bachelor who stays clear of stoves."

At the apartment, I put the groceries away and called Dad to try to find out when Pat's funeral would take place. Since no one answered, I called Diane, the neighbor who had been with him the previous night. "I really appreciate you being there—"

"Haven't you heard?"

"Heard what?"

"Pat's alive."

"She's *what?*"

"The medics were able to get her heart started in the ambulance on the way to the hospital."

"So how is she?" I asked, not sure I wanted to know.

"She's in a coma and connected to a respirator."

"What's the prognosis?"

"No one really knows, but it doesn't look good."

"So she might be in this condition for days or weeks or even years," I said, voicing my worst fears.

"Possibly. No one really knows."

I hung up the phone a bit harder than I intended, thinking that Pat wouldn't want this to happen, because she did everything she could to make life easier for others. *And how am I supposed to live my life when I don't know when her body will cease to function?* I asked myself, for as far as I was concerned, her soul was in a better place.

The phone warbled. It was Jenny asking if I knew anything about the funeral.

"Actually, Pat's still alive," I said. I summarized my conversation with Diane.

"So what am I supposed to do?"

"Hang tight, I guess. I'll call you if I hear something."

"This is ridiculous," she railed. "I'm going to have to find someone to look after my daughter when I'm at the funeral—"

"Of course it's ridiculous," I said. She was a single parent trying to balance work with parenting a fifteen-year-old daughter. "And this is going to be hard on Dad. He's eighty-seven, he has Parkinson's, and he can't drive."

"You're right," she said more calmly. "I'll call him when I get home from work."

"The best we can do is to take this one day at a time; that's what I'm going to try to do."

I hung up the phone, detached Jules from the sofa, put on his harness, and headed to the lobby to work with Shanon for the last time.

"I was going to tell you that my stepmother died last night and ask if Jules should travel with me to the funeral," I told Shanon when we met in the lobby. Once again, Jules's harness was on, his tail was wagging, and my left rear pocket was full of dog treats. "But it turns out she's not dead after all."

"I'm sorry." She paused. "Do you still want to work Jules?"

"Absolutely." Shanon would be leaving in two hours, and I wanted as much support as I could get. And exercising has always been a positive stress outlet.

I worked Jules to the China café, with Shanon shouting an occasional encouraging word from behind. We crossed Calvert Street. We strode through an energizing spring breeze as we crossed the long bridge and four quiet streets. We worked flawlessly through the complicated intersection and strode down Connecticut Avenue toward the café. "Jules, left! To the door!" I encouraged when I thought we were nearing the entrance.

"Way too late," Shanon called with a smile in her voice. She jogged to catch up with us. "Turn around and I'll lead you to a spot where we can try this again."

"Jules, come!" I commanded as I turned around and grabbed onto her left elbow. She guided us to a spot fifty feet from the entrance.

"Let's try this again." We turned around. "Jules, forward! Left, to the door!" He guided me to the correct entrance. "Good boy!" He snatched a treat from my hand as we walked to the counter.

"What do you want?" a woman with a Chinese accent asked from behind the counter.

"Is the special today General Tso's chicken?"

"Yes. You want that with an egg roll and a large ice water?"

"Thanks. Shanon, do you know what you want?"

"Just a minute while I check the menu."

As we ate, I gave her a thumbnail sketch of the progress of Pat's health and asked whether it would be wise to travel with Jules to the funeral in Trenton, New Jersey.

"I'm sure you can handle the trip," she said. "Just give yourself extra time and always keep him with you on-leash."

"I'll do my best," I promised. "And I'm sorry for not attaching Jules to the sofa before you arrived. Keeping him attached to something while not working him has really calmed him down."

"It was a weird moment for me," she confided. "I knew I was right to ask you why Jules was not attached to that sofa." She explained that she had heard good things about my dog-handling skills, and that I was easy to work with. "And then I arrived at your apartment to find him lying on the floor but not attached to anything. I could see that he was bonding well with you, but I wondered what other rules you might be ignoring."

We both laughed. "I made a special effort not to break any more rules after that rebuke."

Back in the apartment lobby, I thanked Shanon for her efforts, and she said that she wished she could drive us to Trenton.

"Don't worry," I told her. "We'll be fine."

"The two of you have a sound relationship," she said as she prepared to leave us for the last time. "You have all the tools you need to be successful so long as you slow down enough to use them."

"I'll do my best." We hugged. "Thanks again for everything."

The following afternoon, Jules and I went to Popeyes for my afternoon meal. The smells of that greasy food wafted from my backpack as we headed back to my apartment. After conquering that three-streets-at-weird-angles intersection, I felt Jules leading me away from the Calvert Street traffic instead of up the street toward Connecticut Avenue.

"Jules, no!" I said, turning us around so that we could walk back to Calvert Street. "We are not visiting the park!"

Upon reaching the corner, I turned so that traffic sounds on Calvert Street were on my left. I commanded Jules to go "forward," and again he veered away from the Calvert Street traffic.

"No!" I said more firmly. I gave him a leash correction. Once again, I worked him to the corner, turned toward home, and encouraged him to go "forward." This time, he made a ninety-degree turn so that we were facing Calvert Street.

"No! We don't want to cross the street," I informed Jules as I faced us in the right direction. "Jules, forward!" Once again, he veered away from the street.

What's wrong with him? I wondered. My stomach rumbled as I worked him back to the corner. I put a foot out tentatively and swept my hands in front of me to see if there might be an obstacle in our path, but all seemed clear. I tried another "forward" command, and he again turned to face Calvert Street.

After fuming to myself for a few seconds, I remembered that I had to use my collapsible white cane as my primary mobility aid when Gifford refused to move forward after a leash correction. "You don't like the way I'm working?" he seemed to be saying with his feet cemented to the ground. "Fine. I'll just stand here and see how you like that!" So I would fish out the cane that I always kept in my backpack ever since the tendon in his right front leg had been sliced in that DC taxi. With a flick of my wrist, the cane would unfold to the ground with a series of five sharp clicks. I would begin walking with my cane in my right hand and Gifford's leash in my left. After about fifty feet, I would pick up the harness and encourage him to go "forward," and after another fifty feet and several encouraging words, we would be walking at our usual brisk pace.

I wondered if this strategy would work with Jules, but just as I began removing the cane from my backpack, a pedestrian asked if I needed help. "Your dog seems confused," he said as Jules pranced, snorted, and wagged his tail.

"No, *I'm* confused. Is Connecticut Avenue in front of me?"

"Yes."

"Are there any obstacles in our way?"

"No; it's clear."

"Jules, forward!" I commanded, but once again he veered away from Calvert Street.

"He's taking you to the park," the stranger called.

"I know," I grumbled, returning to the intersection.

"Do you want me to walk in front of you to see if he might follow me?"

"That would be great!"

"Come on, Jules!" the man said cheerfully.

"Jules, forward!" I mumbled, and he bounded toward the stranger with his tail wagging.

"Thanks," I called after several steps. "We're fine now."

"You sure?"

"Yup. Thanks for the help."

"No problem," the stranger said, and within ten minutes, Jules was attached to the sofa while I devoured my Popeyes feast.

~

EARLY THE FOLLOWING EVENING, I stood in the middle of my apartment struggling to clear my head as WTOP played softly in the background. My warbling phone had jarred me awake from a nap. The call came from Dad, who told me that Pat had died an hour ago and that the funeral would take place at eleven in the morning in two and a half days. Their neighbor Diane had offered to pick me up at the Trenton train station if I could come later that evening. "I don't know if I can with my new dog," I had hedged. "Let me call you back."

Feelings of relief, guilt, and anxiety paralyzed me: relief because Pat was no longer attached to all those tubes; guilt because I thought I should be feeling sad instead of relieved; and anxious because I would soon be traveling to Trenton to attend the funeral and trying to comfort Dad while continuing to strengthen my bond with Jules. I would be taking part in my first funeral for someone close to me, and I didn't quite know what to expect or how I should act. Indeed, a part of me didn't want to go; I dislike ceremonies and worried about the challenges Jules might create. These thoughts increased my guilt and anxiety, which fueled more outlandish thoughts. What if I said or did the wrong thing at the wrong time? What if Jules barked or tried to relieve himself in the middle of the service? What if? What if?

Relax; you can't control your feelings, and there is no right way to feel after someone close to you dies, chided the ghost of my social-work training.

Yes, but what if ... what if?

"It's 6:45," announced the calm authoritative voice of the WTOP newscaster.

I sprang into action. After checking reservation options on Amtrak using its voice mail maze, I realized that I couldn't get to Trenton at a reasonable hour that evening. I called Diane to ask if she could meet me at the station at around 10:30 the next morning. She agreed, so I reentered Amtrak's voice mail maze to book seats for Jules and me. I called my sister, Jenny, and told her that Pat had really died this time and that the funeral would be on Wednesday. She said that she would get there as soon as she could. "And I think you should write a eulogy," she added.

"Me?" I asked, startled.

"Yes. I think Dad would appreciate it."

CHAPTER ELEVEN:
THE TRIP TO TRENTON

~

MARCH 21, 2005

"Let's do it," I said to Jules at 6:30 the next morning. He stretched out on his front legs while his backside vibrated in the air and his tail thudded against the wall. With his harness handle in my left hand, my suitcase in my right hand, and my backpack on my back, we walked out of the apartment building to his park area. After he completed his business, we strode to the Metro station, rode the two escalators down to the station's main level, and walked through the fare gate. I heard distant train sounds from my left as we strode toward the short down-escalator to the platform. I thought we could easily board the train as both Dunbar and Gifford had assisted me onto many trains under similar circumstances. But Jules slowed down as the clattering rumble changed to a shrill squeal, and a spasm of annoyance went through me when it became clear that we would miss this train.

"The two of you have a sound relationship," I remembered Shanon saying to me two days earlier. "You have all the tools you need to be successful so long as you slow down enough to use them."

I took a deep breath. "Good boy, Jules," I told him, and worked him down the short escalator onto the platform once the clattering rumble had faded away.

"Excuse me," I called to a group of strangers as Jules and I stepped off of the next train onto the platform at Union Station. "Which direction is the Amtrak exit?" It was usually to the right, but not always.

"What?"

"The Amtrak exit. Where is it?"

"I don't know."

"There should be a sign somewhere nearby."

"I see it," someone else called. "To the right, about twenty feet."

"Thanks." I turned right and picked up the harness handle. "Jules, forward." We went up a flight of stairs, walked a short distance to an up-escalator, and rode it to the main concourse. We hurried down a long and wide corridor that usually rang with the slap of hurrying feet and buzzing voices but today was quiet due to the early hour. After another right-hand turn and a short walk down another corridor, we ended up at the back of the line of passengers requesting tickets.

"Good morning," the ticket agent said when it was my turn. "How can I help you?"

"I'm here to pick up my ticket for the next train to Trenton." I gave her my name.

"Two tickets?" she asked.

"Yes."

"Where's the other passenger?"

"Right here." I patted Jules's head.

"A dog?"

"Yes. A *guide* dog."

"Sorry. I didn't see her." She paused. "A service animal."

"That's right."

"Hold on." I heard the clatter as she typed on her computer. "There's no charge for a service animal." She handed me tickets and asked if I needed assistance boarding the train. I said yes, and soon I was holding onto the left elbow of another Amtrak employee as he pulled a luggage cart behind him with my suitcase on it. I held Jules's leash with my left hand as we walked down another corridor and stepped onto an escalator that whirred us down from the dry, quiet coolness of the main concourse to the humid, clangy heat of the platform.

"Here we are!" he announced after about another minute's walking. We turned left, stepped over the small crack between the platform and the train, and entered the dry coldness of the empty car. I thanked him as he stowed my luggage in the overhead rack.

"No problem." He turned toward the door. "Nice dog. What's his name?"

"Jules." I sat down and tried to get him to lie down with his head facing forward.

"Nice dog," he repeated. "How long have you had him?"

"This is our third day together."

"Amazing. And he's so well-behaved." He left, letting the door bang shut behind him.

"Jules, down!" I ordered, but he remained standing. "Fine, you can stand for the entire trip for all I care, you silly Labrador," I told him, remembering another piece of Shanon's advice: to let him stand as long as he wasn't bothering other people. Pretending to ignore him, I removed my ticket jacket from my backpack and sat on it so I wouldn't delay the conductor when he came around to collect it. I took out my Braille Lite and headphones and began reading the book I had uploaded to it the previous evening, and within five minutes, Jules had fallen asleep.

"Next stop, Trenton!" the conductor's voice blared over the PA system two hours later. I grabbed my suitcase from the overhead compartment and encouraged Jules to stand up.

"Which way to the main entrance?" I asked the conductor as we prepared to get off.

"Watch out for the gap," he warned.

"Don't worry," I said, remembering a time when I fell through the space between a car and a platform as my sister, Jenny, and I were hurrying to catch a train. Fortunately, the only damages were bruises to both my right knee and my dignity. Jules and I moved cautiously until I felt my foot make contact with the edge.

"Watch out!" the conductor warned again.

"Jules, forward!" We stepped over the gap. "Which way to the main entrance?"

"To the right."

"Thanks." We turned right and began speeding down the platform.

"Peter," called Diane's son, Joey, hurrying to catch up.

"Hey, Joey. Thanks." I grabbed his elbow without slowing down, and we hurried out of the station into the cool, still dampness of the street. "Thanks for the ride," I said to Diane. We hugged one-handed, and she put my suitcase in the trunk of her car.

"How was the trip?" she asked as she pulled out of the parking lot.

I scratched behind Jules's ears. "He did great. He slept during the entire train ride, unlike Gifford, who whined softly whenever he wanted attention from another passenger."

"How's Gifford doing?" Joey asked. He had found Gifford sniffing for food in a Dumpster behind a deli a mile away from Pat's fenced-in backyard. Gifford had seemed quite pleased with his adventure while the rest of us were nervous wrecks after almost losing a dog valued at $50,000.

"He seems to be doing fine." A couple of minutes passed in silence. "Where's Dad?"

"Dr. Altschul is at the church making final arrangements for the funeral," Diane told me.

"Was it lung cancer?" I asked a couple of minutes later.

"Yes, the cancer finally got her."

As the uncomfortable silence continued, I thought about my last serious discussion with Pat about the frustrations of my work life. It was Dad's birthday, and while she began preparing the celebratory dinner, I stood outside the kitchen door and talked about the frustrations of my work at the Maryland office of a large management consulting firm. At first, the job seemed ideal, but it seemed far less attractive after three months of unreturned phone calls, unkept promises, a we-know-everything attitude, and three changes to my start date. I had also learned that their clients were complaining about the way office staff were treating them. And when

I arrived on my first day, my boss didn't remember my name even though she had been part of the interview process.

I spent my first morning organizing my desk, learning how to use the office phone, chatting with some of the staff, and listening to my fellow consultants bitch about their clients. Around noon, one of the office's computer experts showed up to install JAWS onto my computer. She told me that she had been given thirty minutes, and I informed her that more time would likely be needed. The two of us plus Gifford went to the director to explain the situation. She claimed that she was unaware that JAWS might take a while to install, and after an awkward pause, I told her as nicely as I could that I had warned her about possible complications during a phone call and in an e-mail. "You need to be more patient!" she had snapped.

"You shouldn't have said that," Pat had chided gently.

"You're right," I agreed, "but what I really wanted to do was to stalk out of her office and go home. But I let the silence spiral until the director authorized the additional time that would be needed to install the software."

"But why were you so upset with the director?" Pat had probed. "It sounds like she was one of those harried executives who was stressed out. You know the type."

"I do," I said. I had told Pat about how at my first job, stressed-out supervisors blamed the visually impaired employees for their ineptness. If the computer system didn't work, it was because of the technology we used. If they failed to meet their objectives, it was because we burdened the system with too many referrals. "But there's more to it!" I nearly shouted, remembering another lesson learned from my first job. "Customers will sometimes overlook rudeness if they think that the person they're working with is extremely competent, but if they believe that their helper is inept *and* rude, they become pissed. That's what happened to me. I was willing to overlook the director's prior rudeness because I wanted to believe that the higher-ups wouldn't promote an incompetent person to run an office. But at that moment it became clear that she hid her incompetence by being rude and blaming others. No wonder their clients were complaining."

"Why?"

"Because the way employees are treated influences the way they treat others, and employees tend to mimic the behavior of their bosses."

"But aren't you making a lot of assumptions about the director based on such a short conversation?" Pat had asked. "That's not fair, and you're better than that."

"You're right; it's not fair. But I have worked with all kinds of people over the past ten years, and I have pretty good instincts."

As Pat rummaged around a drawer searching for something, I told her that the JAWS installation process had taken twenty-four hours because of conflicts with computer system firewalls. While the computer expert tried to work things out with the manufacturer, I met with my boss for the first time.

"How'd that go?" Pat asked.

"It was bizarre."

"How?"

"After several minutes of getting-to-know-you chitchat, she started criticizing her husband. He was overweight. He was lazy. He didn't like trying new things. And on and on. As the tirade continued, I began wondering why she was dumping all this on me when we barely knew each other. And did she really think that her attitude would encourage him to change? I also couldn't help wondering if she was this contemptuous of all men and how this attitude influenced the way she treated her clients, many of whom were men."

While Pat started chopping something, I told her that once JAWS was installed, I discovered that I could access e-mail but couldn't navigate the organization's internal website because links were not marked in a way that JAWS could "speak" them. The following afternoon, several office employees with computer expertise crowded around my cubicle, and together we summarized the tasks that I couldn't perform: completing human resources paperwork, accessing the templates used to simplify putting together proposals and reports, and entering the on-line library of proposals that others had submitted. "These computer people were bright and committed to their work," I told Pat. "The JAWS software fascinated them, and soon they were able to predict whether or not it could 'read' a given portion of the site. I also began noticing that whenever I reached a spot that JAWS couldn't interpret, these people would criticize the design of that portion of the site."

"Interesting," Pat had said over the sound of running water.

"And while I couldn't understand the jargon, I was happy that these experts were reinforcing my belief that making a site accessible to blind people often makes it easier for others to use."

After e-mailing my boss a summary of my difficulties with the website, I spent the next couple of weeks reviewing material describing the methods they used to assist their clients. In order to stay awake, I eavesdropped on conversations among my fellow consultants about how their clients were stupid, lazy, and inept. "I've done my share of complaining," I said to Pat, "but this carping was relentless. So I quietly talked about this negative chatter with one of the techies who had crowded around my cubicle."

"You don't know what we really do, do you?" he had asked with barely disguised bitterness.

"I guess not."

"We write reports that nobody reads."

"Oh," I muttered. I had written reports that I was sure no one would read as part of my work managing federal grants, but I thought of this activity as a nuisance instead of the main focus of my job.

As I continued to plow through the sleep-inducing material, I began wondering why clients of large management consulting firms would pay such large fees for "reports that nobody reads." Sometimes outside expertise can be really useful, but ...

"And then the answer hit me on the Metro during my trip home," I had told Pat. "They spend this money so that the change *won't* happen."

"What?" she had asked, stopping her kitchen rattling.

"Maybe some executives secretly believe that the change isn't really necessary, but they want to make it seem that they are committed to moving ahead. Others might think that perhaps they should move the organization in a new direction, but a part of them wonders if they can lead others through the turbulence. So they hire one of these large firms who send a team of consultants to lay the groundwork. Team members review documents. They interview employees. They make presentations. Then they prepare a report littered with graphics, charts, pictures, tables, spreadsheets, and time lines detailing the reasons for the needed change, the benefits the change will bring, and a step-by-step process to implement the change. The consulting firm then delivers the document with great fanfare.

"And some executives take one look at the report's size and put it aside. Others start following the recommendations but encounter so much resistance that either the change never happens or the promised benefits fail to take place."

"Why?" Pat had asked.

"Most planned change efforts fail, sometimes because of unexpected shifts in business conditions. Many employees view external consultants as arrogant fools telling them how to run their lives. They wonder why their bosses don't ask them for their ideas instead of wasting money bringing in those outsiders. Given this hostility, even the best change plans are bound to fail."

"I see." Pat had paused to think. "So change efforts often fail despite the best efforts of well-meaning people."

"It's worse than that." I was on a roll now. "I think these management consulting firms are enabling; you remember reading those social work articles about how well-meaning family and friends enable the substance-abuser to continue drinking or drugging or whatever by making excuses for them or cleaning up their messes?"

"How could I forget?"

"I think these management consultants, perhaps subconsciously, enable the senior executives they work with to continue doing the things that got them into trouble. So instead of encouraging them to change their behavior, they promise to do all the work. When the change fails, the executives can pretend to blame the consultants for not doing what they promised, and the consultants can pretend to blame the executives for not following their instructions. Money changes hands, and the status quo is preserved!"

"I wonder if I should discuss this with my boss," I had said half-seriously.

"No!" Pat had nearly shouted. "They won't hear you."

I knew she was right, but still …

"Please don't," Pat had repeated more quietly, and I agreed.

"And please give this more time," she had coaxed. "Things might get better." But things went from bad to worse, and I left the office for the last time on a warm, breezy day, happy to get back to my more relaxed and productive life.

As Diane drove her car into the gravel driveway of Pat's large, airy three-story house by the Delaware River, a wave of sadness rolled over me as I realized how much I had grown to depend on her empathic intelligence and her ability to ask tough questions in a gentle voice. This wise warmth would be hard to replace.

The barks of the toy poodle greeted us as we got out of the car. "Happy, no!" Pat's live-in housekeeper, Pamela, ordered from the other side of the screen door.

"Hi, Pam, how you doing?" I called. Diane handed me my suitcase. Jules and I walked into the house as Happy growled from Pamela's arms.

"Oh fine, fine," she said tonelessly.

"So how are things?" I repeated after Diane had left.

"Oh, fine." Happy grumbled quietly from Pamela's arms as Jules panted with excitement at the chance to meet a new dog. "I just can't believe she's gone."

"I can't either," I said, thinking that while I had known Pat since 1969, Pamela had been her live-in housekeeper since the mid-1960s. They had first met while Pat served as a diplomat's wife in India. Pat had offered her a job, and she had left her family and flown to the United States with Pat. They had been together ever since.

"I think I'll go upstairs and unpack," I mumbled after an awkward pause that I was sure Pat would have handled gracefully.

As Jules and I walked up the thirteen carpeted stairs, I remembered the many times during the past twenty-five years when I had run up and down those stairs with my guide dogs thundering behind. "Here comes the herd of elephants," Pamela had called as Pat's toy dogs would yap or grumble indignantly. After unpacking, I heeled Jules downstairs and through the kitchen, where Pamela was watching a soap opera on a small television set.

"I'm taking Jules outside to park," I told her as Happy grumbled from her lap.

"Get busy," I encouraged as we strolled toward Pat's swimming pool with birds chirping to my left and traffic roaring by on the right. As he sniffed out his new park area, I smiled, remembering how Pamela and Pat worked together in the kitchen to prepare all those wonderful meals that kept me well-fed and open to Pat's wisdom. They both loved to play the New York State lottery, and family friends were afraid that Pamela might retire after she won nearly a million dollars. But she didn't even think of leaving despite the occasional arguments that would flare up between them and then blow over like a fast-moving thunderstorm. Their love for each other was just too strong.

Back in Pat's kitchen, I decided to give Jules a taste of freedom; after all, he had relieved himself in a new park area after our first successful trip together. I was confident that he would not bother Happy because Heidi, Nan, Dunbar, and Gifford had ignored Tarzan, Michelle, Poppy, and Happy. I knew that Guiding Eyes discouraged this, but I was an experienced dog handler. So I asked Pamela if she would mind if I let Jules run free for a few minutes.

"No, that's fine."

"Is any of Happy's food lying around?" I asked, recalling how my prior guide dogs would remove any leftover steak, lamb chops, or chicken from unguarded plates with one swipe of their tongues.

"No, the food plate is safe."

I took off Jules's leash, and he bounded after Happy from the dining room to the living room with his feet sliding across the carpet. Happy, barking indignantly, tried to escape. "Jules, come!" I commanded. "Happy, come here!" Pamela called. Jules spied the basket in which Happy's toys were stored and began scattering them throughout the living room as Happy barked more loudly. "Happy, come here!" Pamela shouted, chasing her. "Jules, come!" I commanded from the entrance of the living room. "Jules, *come!*" I shouted, and miraculously, he obeyed. "Good boy!" I exclaimed as I put the leash on him. "Good girl!" Pamela said, stooping down to pick up Happy.

"I'm sorry," I said as Jules panted and wagged his tail. "I didn't expect him to cause such chaos."

"That's all right." Pamela laughed as Happy continued to grumble from her arms. "I didn't expect him to want to play with Happy."

"I didn't either." I turned toward the stairs. "And I'm sorry he trashed Happy's toy basket."

Pamela continued to chuckle. "Don't worry. I'll pick the toys up later."

So Jules and I, energized and amused, walked back upstairs, leaving a grumpy Happy in Pamela's arms and toys for her to retrieve.

CHAPTER TWELVE:
THE EULOGY

~

MARCH 21–24, 2005

everal minutes later, a volley of indignant yaps and the slamming of the screen door alerted me to the arrival of my dad.

"Hi, Dr. Altschul," Pamela called as I put the leash back on Jules and hurried downstairs.

"Hi, Dad," I said. "How did the funeral preparations go?"

"Oh fine," he mumbled, heading toward the den with Jules and me in tow. He launched into a tirade about dealing with the funeral details. When he had wound down, I encouraged him to say hello to Jules. His greeting was so flat that Jules didn't wag his tail. Surprised, I asked what was wrong. "Nothing," he groused, and continued his rant about funeral details. When he wound down again, I asked if he had heard from Jenny.

"Yes," he said. "Let me see. She said she would arrive sometime this evening." He paused. "And we talked about something else."

"Something about a eulogy?" I prompted.

"Yes, she said something about that."

"Would you like me to do that?"

"Very much," he said, "and you need to call the priest who will be conducting the funeral. I have his name and phone number somewhere." He rifled through his pockets. "Here it is," he said, handing me a small crumpled piece of paper. "Can you get Pamela to read this to you so you can put it on your Braille Lite? I would do it, but—"

"I know," I interrupted, not wanting him to have to admit that he could no longer help me with clerical details. "I'll take care of it."

I stood in the doorway, not knowing what I could say to make things a little better for both of us. "I'm sorry" seemed trite, since I had said this twice to him already. Other traditional phrases also seemed out of place, as both of us found them to be more annoying than comforting. Over the years, I had experienced the healing power of a hug, but the only time I had touched Dad was when I held onto his elbow so he could assist me to where I wanted to go. He touched me through his resonant voice, his infectious laugh, his wry wit, his restless intellect, his ability to convey a point through a well-told story, his shrewd observations about workplace politics, and his commitment to do the right thing well, but he rarely touched me with his hands. And we rarely talked about feelings.

I heard the rustle of a newspaper. "I guess I'll have to start working on that eulogy," I said, backing out of the door and slouching upstairs with Jules by my side.

But I didn't. Instead, I chatted with Dad about sports during lunch, and spent the rest of the afternoon reading and napping in my room with Jules attached to a chair at the foot of the bed. Diane, her husband, Scott, and Joey joined us for dinner, and Jules's thumping tail and Happy's barks signaled the arrival of other neighbors who talked of Pat's generosity and offered their support. Jenny arrived and worked her way around the table, hugging everybody and thanking them for coming. "Hi, Pete," she said when she arrived at my chair. We hugged as Jules's tail thumped on the rug. She knelt beside him. "Hi, Jules. You're very handsome." He rolled on his back and snorted as Happy barked from the kitchen.

"Happy, you're jealous," Jenny and Pamela said together, and all of us laughed.

"Did Dad ask you to write the eulogy?" Jenny asked as the conversation picked up around us.

"Yes."

"Have you started working on it yet?"

"No. I'll work on it tomorrow morning."

But I didn't. Instead, Jenny and I took Jules on a one-mile route around the quiet streets of the neighborhood. Working a guide dog every day is especially important early in the relationship so that the team can continue to learn to work together. Like Shanon, Jenny walked several feet behind me, cheering us on and warning me of some small danger ahead.

Dad had been an ideal substitute guide dog trainer and walking companion for fifteen years. He loved dogs and was fascinated with animal behavior. He had a great sense of direction and could communicate directions clearly. He loved to walk and could match my four-mile-per-hour pace because of his soccer-playing, long-distance running, and mountain climbing while growing up in Dusseldorf, Germany, during the 1920s and 1930s. Every morning after breakfast, we would walk two-mile routes around the neighborhood in all kinds of weather, talking about sports, politics, money, or neighborhood gossip while Pat slept. When we returned, he would head upstairs to receive his marching orders from Pat, often accompanied by volleys of shrill yaps from one of their toy dogs. Occasionally, one of my dogs would barge into their room and steal food, prance around or on their bed, or vomit on their thick carpet. Pat had always accepted my embarrassed apology and ended up using these experiences as the basis of a song we wrote together, which was performed twice at New England Conservatory.

While my walks with Dad had ended ten years earlier because he could no longer keep up with me, we continued our lively man-to-man conversations during phone calls and in-person whenever Pat wasn't around. But it hadn't been quite the same; I had moved to DC, and his intellectual stamina was slowly wearing down.

Happy's shrill yaps greeted us when Jenny and I returned from our walk. As she talked with Dad in the dining room, I took off Jules's harness and called the priest who would be leading the funeral mass the following day.

"Hello, Father," I said when he came to the phone. "I'm Pat Altschul's stepson, and I'm hoping you won't mind me delivering a eulogy as part of the service?"

"Must you?" he whined.

"Yes," I shot back. "I must."

"Well, no more than five minutes, please," he snapped before slamming down the phone.

"What do you mean, 'if you must'?" I said to Jenny and Dad after relating the conversation during lunch.

Jenny snorted. "What's his problem?"

"I have no idea, but I hope he isn't like those priests at the Catholic church I attended while in high school."

"Why didn't I know about this?" Dad asked. He had told us about a Lutheran pastor hitting him hard on the head with the bow of a cello because he couldn't sing in tune. He also resented the German Lutheran Church's support of Hitler during his rise to power.

"This happened after the divorce," I explained. "I sang with a bunch of high school friends every Sunday for a year and a half in a folk group that provided the music for the noon mass. You remember, don't you?" I asked Jenny.

"No," she confessed. "I slept until noon most weekends."

I talked about how a high school classmate with a friendly female voice recruited me to join the group during my sophomore year. "I really enjoyed the rehearsals," I said, "because I could shine in front of several girls with sexy voices. But during the actual masses, the priests raced through the liturgy with the ruthless efficiency of a fast-moving assembly line. Their flat robotic voices sounded rather like my Braille Lite." Jenny and Dad laughed loudly. "So the experience was valuable, but the priests' monotonous drone made it impossible to experience any sort of divine presence."

We spoke about Pat's pride in her Catholic heritage, how she regularly attended Mass, and her irritation with the church's stance toward women. I heard Dad start to laugh, which was odd because the conversation wasn't funny. But then I realized he wasn't laughing at all. He was weeping.

I sat in my chair as Jenny hurried around the table to hug him. I couldn't move. It was the first time I had heard him cry.

"It's okay," Jenny said from beside Dad's chair. "We're here for you."

"That's right," I babbled, my social-work side taking over. "We all miss Pat, and we'll do what we can to help you get through this."

"I'm sorry," he said after he had calmed down.

"For what?" Jenny and I asked together.

"For breaking down in front of you; it's embarrassing."

We hurried to tell him not to worry, that this was a tough time for all of us, and that Pat was a special person. "We need to stick together," Jenny said as we all got up from the table.

"So are you going to work on the eulogy this afternoon?" Jenny asked as Dad left the room for his afternoon nap.

"I don't know; maybe," I hedged.

But I didn't, choosing instead to watch an episode of a soap opera, read a magazine, eat dinner, and veg in front of sports talk radio.

"The funeral's tomorrow," Jenny said in exasperation as we prepared to go to bed. "Have you written anything yet?"

"Don't worry; I'll take care of it," I mumbled.

The next morning, I woke up at 5:30 to the sound of rain clattering against the window. I tuned the radio to WCBS News Radio 88, took my Braille Lite out of my backpack, and began writing.

"At the tone, the time will be seven a.m.," announced the news anchor as Jenny tapped on the door and Jules shook himself. "Come in. I've just about finished," I called quietly.

"Hi, Jules. You're awfully cute," she cooed, closing the door behind her. "But why are you trying to walk between my legs?"

"He does that all the time; it's a game."

After they settled down, I began reading what I had written. Jenny was pleased, but caught a couple of convoluted sentences and grammatical missteps. We laughed and shared memories as Jules rolled on his back and hiccupped.

During the next two hours, Jenny and I took showers, ate breakfast, and put on the clothes we would be wearing to the funeral. Happy kept up a stream of indignant barking, heralding the arrival of Pat's friends from Trenton and New York City.

"Do we really need to take Jules?" Jenny asked as I dressed him in his harness.

"Absolutely." We began walking down the stairs to greet Pat's friends. "I'm sure she would want him there."

As we mingled with the guests near the front door, Jules stood with his tail gently wagging as Pat's friends fussed over him.

"He's lovely," somebody said. "Pat would have been so pleased."

"I'm sure you're right."

An old family friend asked if he had ever gone to church.

"I don't know," I answered, "but did I ever tell you what happened when I took Heidi to church for the first time?"

"I don't think so."

"There was this Lutheran church near my Manhattan apartment that I had always wanted to check out. So one Sunday morning, Heidi and I showed up there. We were warmly welcomed, and soon I was talking with two nice ladies as Heidi dozed under the pew. After the opening hymn and welcoming announcements, the pastor began praying for one of the church members. He talked of knowing this person since she was in grammar school and how she had grown through her high school and college experiences."

"The limo's here," Jenny called.

"Then the pastor explained that this longtime church member would be leaving soon to attend seminary," I continued as Pamela and Jenny began helping Dad toward the front door. "After he described some of the challenges she might face, the pastor paused for dramatic effect."

"Peter, we're going to be late!" Jenny called.

"And so," I said, mimicking the pastor's rich voice, "we ask you, Lord, to watch over Heidi—

"And Heidi the Weimaraner leapt to her feet and shook herself, and no one around me heard the rest of the prayer."

"'No, Heidi,' I had grunted as the people sitting around me snorted. 'He's not talking to you. Lie down!'"

My Trenton audience laughed as we all left the house to walk toward the limo. Dad, Jenny, Jules, and I settled into its tomb-like quietness as the others got into their cars to follow us for the ten-minute drive to the church.

We settled into our assigned pew in the front row, with Dad sitting between Jenny and me with Jules sprawled underneath. Several minutes later, quiet chords from the organ signaled the start of the service. We all stood up.

"The casket's coming," Jenny whispered in my ear. Dad began weeping again. I tentatively put my hand on his shoulder, and he regained his composure as we were told to sit. The priest hurried through the service in a flat voice. A small group of women sang the responses in tune but without warmth.

Jenny poked me lightly in the ribs thirty minutes later. "You're after this prayer," she whispered. As the priest sped through the prayer of comfort in a robotic drone, I roused myself from a disgusted trance and checked my Braille Lite to be sure that the eulogy was ready to be read. When the priest finished, Jenny, Jules, and I headed to the podium. "Here we are," she whispered. She put the Braille Lite on top of the podium, put my right hand on the microphone, and returned to her seat.

"Jules, down," I whispered.

The tags on Jules's collar rattled as he shook his head.

"Jules, down!" I whispered more urgently.

"Hurry up," Jenny hissed.

"Jules, down!" I pleaded, but he didn't budge.

Shanon had suggested that I let Jules stand as long as he wasn't bothering other people, so I put my right foot on his leash, turned on my Braille Lite, and started reading.

"Good morning," I began tentatively. "My name is Peter Altschul, and I am proud to be Pat's stepson. But this was not always true.

"When I first met her in 1969, I was a twelve-year-old brat. You know about teenage boys: prone to making lots of noise, consuming prodigious quantities of food, and causing chaos. These traits were bound to conflict with the calm elegant atmosphere that she aimed to create. And the mythic 'evil stepmother' is a hard thing to overcome."

I talked about how Pat had won us over by serving us wonderful food and taking us to Broadway shows, sporting events, and even amusement parks, where she had ridden on one of the faster roller coasters.

"I must confess," I continued, "that while I welcomed her efforts, I didn't fully appreciate her specialness. But several of my high school and college lady friends did, and *that* got my attention."

I described our efforts as a songwriting team. I talked about how Pat assisted in my pursuit of a master's in social work by reading articles onto cassettes, and how she encouraged my efforts at assisting groups and organizations in working across boundaries to accomplish something worthwhile. "I learned far more from Pat about influencing others than from books," I added.

After thanking Pat for being such a good wife to our dad, I reminded the audience that she had a special gift for hospitality, which showed itself not just by the parties she organized and the meals she served but also by steering conversations so that everybody could participate and discouraging snide comments about people or dogs we didn't like. She had the knack of making people feel better about themselves, offering encouraging words and hugs.

"And now Pat is gone," I rhapsodized, "to a place where people cooperate instead of compete and where dogs, cats, and other animals are welcome on buses, trains, and planes, as well as in restaurants, theaters, stores, taxis, and places of worship.

"Yes gone, but not forgotten," I continued, becoming aware of quiet titters from some in the audience. "I will remember Pat while eating a good meal, upon the onset of the first snow, and while working with my guide dog." The tittering increased. "I will miss her generous hugs, wonderful laugh, sense of adventure, intellectual curiosity, and her words of wisdom. I will remember her while trying to make the world a better place for the less fortunate. And of course, I will miss her wonderful meals and hospitality."

The tittering grew louder.

"I am proud to be her stepson," I declared. "Farewell, Pat, and thank you for making this world, especially my world, a better place."

The room was still as I turned off my Braille Lite and waited for Jenny to help me back to my seat.

"What was Jules doing?" I whispered as we eased into the pew.

"He was sniffing one of the nuns."

After the service, we passed a small group of people milling around the lobby. "They're waiting for us to leave so their funeral service can begin," Jenny explained as we got back into the limo for the short drive to a local restaurant for lunch.

The mood inside the restaurant was a mixture of sadness and edginess. Many of Pat's friends came up to the head table to comfort Dad and to thank me for the eulogy, saying that it was the only part of the Mass that seemed real. Several people talked about how the service's sterile coldness was an insult to Pat's warmth and generosity. "This is one of the reasons I left the priesthood!" fumed one of Pat's former neighbors whom I had met twenty-five years earlier along with his wife and four-year-old son while visiting Dad and Pat. Since none of us were hungry, large containers of hearty Italian food joined us in the limo for the drive back to the house, which soon was full of loud chatter and Happy barks.

After chatting with the guests, Jules and I escaped upstairs, where I changed from the dark suit I had worn to the funeral to more comfortable clothes. Our trip to Jules's park area was interrupted by a greeting from one of Pat's New York City friends.

"Hi, Stephanie," I called. She lived in the same building as Pat and had befriended all of my prior guide dogs.

"Jules looks good," she said from the bottom of the stairs. "He even walks like you."

I reached the bottom of the stairs and stopped. "What do you mean?"

She paused for a moment. "He matches your pace perfectly."

"He does," I agreed. "There isn't much tension on the leash when we walk together, unlike Heidi who never heeled."

We laughed. "Heidi was the perfect dog for you then," Stephanie said, "because you were both impatient."

As Jules stood by my side, we began sharing Heidi memories: how Stephanie had retrieved her from the lobby of Pat's apartment building after she had darted through the door of an open elevator on the sixth floor; how people would dive out of our way as Heidi and I prowled the crowded Manhattan sidewalks; how she had dragged me out of the path of an ambulance that silently cut in front of us when the light was in our favor; how she had shredded a stuffed animal that Stephanie had given her on Christmas Eve; how Pat had nursed her back to health after a stray dog had attacked her; and how during one of Pat's Christmas parties, she had drained the glass of an unsuspecting guest that had contained a cocktail that Pat had made in his honor.

Jenny joined us, drawn by our laughter, and the conversation veered to Heidi's antics at the Aspen Music Festival: how her uncropped tail had swatted a newly opened can of beer from the table as she charged through the room, leaving behind a stunned silence and mounds of foam; how she had added to the atmosphere of a performance of a piece I had written for voice and bassoon by snapping at a mosquito; how she had tried to persuade the wife of my composition teacher through impassioned barks and howls that she should give her the hot dog the woman was holding; and how Heidi had mirrored my irritation at having to sit through a live performance of a Bruckner symphony by, as the woman sitting next to me had put it, "assiduously sniffing the behind of the person sitting in front of us."

As Jules and I walked through the kitchen to the park area, I sensed Pat more clearly through sharing those Heidi stories than during that antiseptic church service or even while writing and delivering the eulogy, which, while from the heart, seemed contrived. I reflected that funerals, weddings, and other ceremonies can be powerful catalysts toward healing and renewal, but only if they connect with the beliefs, feelings, and experiences of those in attendance.

~

THE HOUSE FELT EMPTY WHEN Diane arrived to drive Jules and me to the train station the following afternoon. Jenny had driven Dad to a medical appointment an hour earlier. Pamela was watching television in the kitchen. Even Happy seemed subdued.

During the drive to the station, I thought about the relaxing summer weekends my guide dogs and I had spent at Pat's swimming pool, where

I perfected my cannonball technique, talked with Dad while lying in the sun, and enjoyed Pat's poolside feasts. Meanwhile, Heidi would stalk birds and tree squirrels, unearth moles, or steal food while staying as far away from the pool as possible so she wouldn't get wet. Nan the chocolate Lab would join me in the pool, sometimes scratching me in her excitement, while Dunbar and Gifford seemed happy to lie in the sun surveying their surroundings. Pat and the dogs became friends because of her gentle voice and the smell of food that always seemed to be around her. As Diane turned into the train station, it hit me that Jules and I would probably never hang out at that pool together, for I was certain that Dad would want to sell the house and live a quieter life in the Manhattan apartment that Pat and he had shared for more than thirty years.

Jules slept under the seat as the Amtrak train brought us back to the life we had started together twelve days earlier in Washington, DC. I couldn't concentrate on the book I was reading, so I took off my headphones and let my mind wander. I missed Pat and worried about Dad's future without her. While I was proud of my professional successes, I feared that my relationship with my two top clients would end within a year. As the train screeched into Union Station, I sensed that something about my ordered life needed to change. I somehow knew that a Dunbar Factor was heading my way, and hoped that I would be ready to allow it to lead me forward.

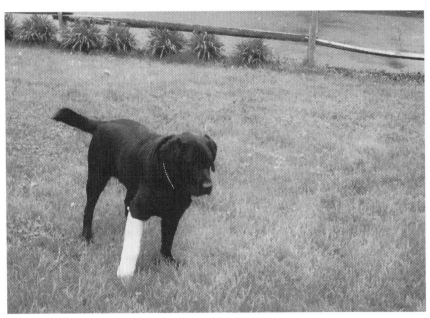

Gifford in cast; April, 2000

PART IV:

~

SAYING HELLO

CHAPTER THIRTEEN:
WHAT HAPPENS IN VEGAS …

APRIL–SEPTEMBER 2005

During the next three months, Jules and I settled into my urban bachelor lifestyle. Every morning, he would greet me by slithering headfirst between my legs, wagging his tail while I muttered endearments and drummed on his hindquarters. Every day, we walked together for at least a mile, and over time, he grew to understand that I wanted to return to my apartment after visiting Popeyes instead of the local park. Within a month, he had learned to find the door to the China Café, as well as entrances to other restaurants, stores, and apartment buildings. He had learned to pull over to a curb whenever he had to get busy, but not until he had tried to poop in the middle of Park Avenue during a Manhattan rush hour while we were hurrying to a hotel from an unsuccessful job interview. "No!" I had implored, somehow getting us across the street before taking off his harness so he could get busy in peace.

He became a regular fixture at the boys'-night-out get-togethers, lying under the table and ignoring the raucous clatter around him. We took the Metro to the large NGO, where his good looks, wagging tail, and quiet cheerfulness won him many admirers as I wrapped up my work there.

We rode Amtrak to visit New York City, where I continued to manage the Reverse Mentoring Program for that London-based corporation. He assisted in my efforts to sell myself during several job interviews, but while the hiring managers were amazed at our abilities, they always hired someone else.

In mid-April, Jenny and I spent several days in Manhattan looking after Dad while Pamela was visiting relatives in India. It soon became clear that Pat had shielded us from Dad's failing health, and his frail condition hit me like a slap in the face. He could barely walk the short distance between living room, kitchen, dining room, and bedroom. He was rapidly losing his once-prodigious short-term memory and could no longer do battle with bureaucrats over the phone. As he listened from his chair, I spent many hours with his cordless phone nestled between ear and shoulder fighting his battles connected with putting the Trenton house on the market, making arrangements for his care, and beginning to organize Pat's estate. Back in DC, I spoke with him and his caregivers almost every day and continued my advocacy efforts on his behalf. "You're doing good," he always said. "I taught you well." I would always smile and thank him, for I had learned how to address faceless bureaucrats firmly but kindly by watching him in action. And like any good teacher, he was quick to congratulate a student for learning his lesson well.

In early July, I flew to Las Vegas to attend the annual convention of the American Council of the Blind (ACB for short). I had attended these conventions since the late 1980s after several of my visually impaired friends had encouraged me to join. Over the years, I grew to admire its efforts to improve living conditions of blind people through supporting the passage of the Americans with Disabilities Act and other legislation. They also encourage businesses, schools, social service agencies, and other organizations to improve the way they work with blind people as well as providing information, guidance, and encouragement to members. I traveled without Jules; while he was developing into a sound guide and wonderful companion, I had grown to dislike bringing my dogs to these conventions because of the hectic schedule, cramped quarters, the swinging canes of participants, and the presence of more than three hundred other guide dogs. So I left him behind, confident that Gifford and the Walters would take good care of him.

Like other large conferences, the ACB convention is a mix of business meetings, workshops, exhibits, receptions, and tours. Over the years, I had assisted in forming a committee to address the challenges that we face while trying to land and keep a job. I had also joined Friends-in-Art (FIA), a small group of blind musicians, writers, sculptors, painters, and others to encourage museums to become more blind-friendly and to work with designers of popular music-related hardware and software to make their products more user-friendly for blind musicians. FIA also conducts several workshops at these conventions and puts on an annual popular variety show known as The Showcase of the Performing Arts.

At around ten o'clock on a Sunday evening, I headed to a dance to hear a friend perform. As I approached the door using his singing voice as a beacon, I was stopped by a hug.

"Pee-ter!" a woman squealed.

Startled, I hugged back, thinking that the voice might belong to a woman I had met at last year's ACB convention who was legally but not totally blind.

"Lisa?"

"Yes! How *are* you?"

"Lisa?" an unfamiliar male voice called from somewhere.

"Go into the room," she said to me, "and I'll join you."

I walked through the door toward the singing with my cane bouncing off tables and chairs. "Hey, Gordon," I called between songs. I listened for the clinking bottles that would signal the location of the bar, but after a couple of minutes of fruitless searching, I sat down in an empty chair and began relaxing to Gordon's grooves.

As he worked his magic, I thought about my first meeting with Lisa in Birmingham, Alabama. I had been gossiping with Donna, the wife of the then second vice president at a mixer hosted by ACB's Alaska affiliate.

"Babe?" her husband had called from across the room.

"Over here, Mitch," we had called back.

"Peter! Just the person I wanted to talk to," he had drawled as he came toward us. He told me I needed to meet an ACB scholarship winner named Lisa, a nurse working toward her PhD in biomedical engineering at the University of Missouri. "She's married with three kids and worked for the Al Gore 2000 presidential campaign!" he had finished, his voice rippling with excitement.

"I'd be happy to meet her," I had said, amused by his bubbly voice. I had grown to admire his unflappable but friendly professionalism and his dry sense of humor. His voice had faded away as he melted back into the crowd.

"Lisa, this is my wife Donna," he had said when they joined us. "And here's Peter."

I moved my hand in her general direction. "Hi."

Her cool hand grasped mine. "Hi," she had said in a warm, enthusiastic voice. "Mitch has been telling me all about you."

"And he told me a little about you. I must confess that I have never met a nurse engineer parent who found the time to work for a political campaign."

A few minutes later, we headed to a reception hosted by computer enthusiasts. On the way, Lisa explained that she had been a nurse until 2000 when a rare eye disease had led to her blindness.

"But you have some vision," I had guessed, not hearing the tapping of a cane or the jangling of a dog in harness.

"Yes, I can see just enough to be dangerous," she trilled.

As we walked toward the new reception, she talked about working toward her PhD and of her love of her kids and her respect for Al Gore. While her words were interesting, it was her voice that grabbed my attention. It suggested warmth and humor and intelligence and enthusiasm and hot sex and a love of life. As the four of us entered the noisy room where the new reception was taking place, I thought that while she was incredible, she was, unfortunately, married.

For the next half hour, the four of us continued our conversation fueled by more alcohol, pretzels, and chips until I announced that I had to attend a chorus rehearsal. I went on to explain that every year, about twenty singers got together to perform an original arrangement of a Friends-in-Art member.

"So you sing?" Lisa had asked.

"Not really. I mean, I have a good voice for a chorus—"

"But you're singing something tomorrow night during the show, aren't you?" Donna had interrupted. "And you're the drummer in the house band that backs up many of the performers."

"Yes," I had conceded. I have never been comfortable talking about my successes. "Nobody likes someone who talks about themselves all the time; listen to what others have to say," Mom would snap whenever she thought I was getting too full of myself. Over the years, I had learned that keeping a low profile, listening to others, and letting my skills do the talking allowed me to influence corporate executives, political activists, angry customers, New York City taxi drivers, and young adults to move in a better direction. And sharing my successes too early in an encounter often resulted in either stunned silence or a torrent of praise during which the phrases "you're amazing" or "you're such an inspiration" were almost always included.

"So you *do* sing," Lisa had exclaimed. "I might have to come to the show."

Lisa and I hugged as we said our good-byes, and from the hug, I learned that she was almost as tall as me and in good physical shape. But she was married.

The following evening, the four of us had met again at a reception for those who had performed in the showcase. While drinking cheap wine and gorging on junk food, we had gossiped about the performers who were good and those who weren't; Gordon's successful marriage proposal in the middle of the show to Janiece, a talented singer and pianist; his frustration with the technical glitches—

"But you *can* sing," Lisa had exclaimed in a faintly accusatory voice.

"Thanks, I guess—"

"And I love the song you sang. Billy Joel? 'Goodnight, Saigon?'"

"That's right. I was reminded of it while attending the Broadway show *Movin' Out* with my stepmother last spring. And it seemed appropriate because of our invasion of Afghanistan and Iraq."

As the reception continued, the four of us became more raucous until Gordon, whose room was attached to the suite, declared that it was "two o'clock in the fucking morning" and that he needed some sleep.

"Sorry, Gord," Mitch and I had mumbled.

"Good night, Gord," Donna and Lisa had warbled as we careened out of the room, down the hall, and into the elevator.

Lisa and I hadn't spoken to each other since.

"I'm taking a break after this song," Gordon announced twenty minutes after I had sat in that random chair. As he sang "Disco Inferno," I thought that this wasn't the first time a woman had stood me up. I had engaged in a long-distance relationship with another woman with three kids ten years earlier that had ended badly. "And Lisa was married," I reminded myself as I stood up to leave.

"Pee-ter," Lisa squealed, hurrying to my side. "I'm so sorry. Everybody's been talking, and I haven't been able to—"

"Where's the bar?" I interrupted.

After a couple of quick drinks and an intoxicating slow dance, I held onto her elbow. As we wandered around the hotel, she described her life as a PhD candidate and mother, and I did everything I could to keep her talking so I could savor her warm, enthusiastic voice. We stopped in a quiet place for a romantic hug.

We broke apart. "This hotel sucks," she said.

I found her hand, and we continued strolling. "Yeah, it's noisy and confusing, and I'm always getting lost."

"And it stinks of ancient puke, booze, and cigarette smoke."

Our passion for each other mushroomed as we meandered toward my hotel room. We kissed in the elevator and again outside the door.

"I have a roommate," I told her, eager for action but uncomfortable with getting it on with a married woman.

"So do I." She seemed both sorry and relieved.

I fumbled for my key. "Good night."

Lisa turned toward the elevator. "Good night."

Two nights later, she found me at the reception for those who had performed in the Friends-in-Art Showcase. Once again, I had been the drummer of the house band and had sung in the chorus. Our conversation was interrupted by the arrival of the house band's guitar player and a singer with a reputation as a gifted womanizer. They were both interested in Lisa, and I was too tired to compete. But I found myself walking through the casino's cacophony, listening to the mating calls of her suitors. As the courting continued at one of the hotel bars, I leaned back in my chair wondering who would win. But they left some time later ... and Lisa was still there.

She turned toward me. "Thank God they're gone."

I grunted.

"Nice houses, nobody home."

"Who? The people who left?"

She put her hand on my knee. "Weren't they in the showcase?"

I told Lisa that the guitar player had been playing in the house band for several years and that the singer had been an audience favorite for as long as I could remember. Since she hadn't attended the show, I talked about the parts that rocked and those that fell flat. I told her that being a part of the house band was one of the high points every year because I had the chance to work with gifted musicians over a two-day period to prepare to back up as many as ten singers. "It's stressful and exhilarating, but I always feel tired and a bit let down after it's over."

Lisa said she understood.

"And I'm surprised you're still here," I confessed.

"What?" She removed her hand from my knee. "No! I want to be with you."

I lamely apologized and began talking about the love wars I had lost in high school and college—

"Where did you go to school?" she interrupted.

I told her reluctantly, as disclosing this information usually resulted in disbelieving clucks, disinterest, or over-the-top praise.

"Princeton!" she exclaimed, and for the next several minutes we compared notes about our college days. Suddenly a bolt of inspiration struck me.

"What's wrong?" Lisa asked.

"Nothing. I was wondering if you might want to come with me to the FIA board dinner tomorrow night. It's my last night here, and I thought—"

"Sure! I'd love to!"

We met at the FIA suite the next evening and headed to the bar for a quick drink. We railed against the raucous glitziness of Las Vegas. We talked about what we had done during the convention. Suddenly another bolt of inspiration struck me.

"What's wrong?" Lisa asked.

"Nothing. I wondered if I could have your phone number and e-mail address." I figured we could still be friends even though she was married.

"I would love to hear from you," she gushed, so we exchanged contact information before strolling hand in hand to an overpriced, mediocre Italian restaurant near the hotel to join the rest of the FIA board. We talked about haiku, Buddhism, the arts, politics, and our careers with a young, recently married couple. After they left, Lisa talked about her challenges as the only visually impaired student in the University of Missouri's engineering school. I told her about a meeting that had taken place two months earlier connected with the Reverse Mentoring Program.

"I was in the office of my boss's new boss talking about the program," I said, "when he interrupted to ask what it was like to work there as a blind man."

"What did you say?"

"I didn't want to talk about my sometimes frustrating but usually positive relationship with the organization with a senior HR person who I barely knew. So I mumbled that things were going well despite some earlier difficulties and went back to my presentation. And then he interrupted again to tell me that he was fifty-something years old and gay."

"What?"

"And then he told me about how the phone rang during the interview for his current job and that he had overheard his interviewer making snide comments about his sexual orientation and how he had told the interviewer that he would sue if he wasn't hired."

"And they hired him?"

170

"Obviously. What idiots."

"I think he was trying to connect with you."

"How?"

"You are both members of groups who are discriminated against?"

"I'm sure you're right, but he came across as an angry, white gay guy."

Lisa laughed. "Aren't you being a bit harsh?"

"If we're going to call certain African Americans 'angry black men,' then it seems fair to label members of other groups who act the same way."

Lisa laughed again. "Angry, white gay guy—I love it!"

We held hands as I talked about my first two bosses there. The first was a white, middle-aged woman whose father had recently become blind. While this connection helped me get the job, she began complaining that I was far more independent than her father. And she was often unavailable when I could have used her guidance, either because of other commitments or because of the crippling headaches she endured due to a prior stroke. She was forced to resign eighteen months after I was hired, in part because the only person on her staff who liked her was a white woman. The rest of us—an African American woman, two Latinas, and I—had begun bombarding her boss with complaints.

"I'm sorry she was let go," I confided. "Unlike my other inept bosses, I liked her. We would have supported her better if she had told us how we could adapt to her disability. She had difficulty working with people from different backgrounds. But I wish I had done a better job reaching out to her."

I told Lisa that my second boss was a white man who tried to mask his insecurity with bombast, bluster, and blaming others for his mistakes, and within a year, he had forced out everybody except the white woman.

Lisa snorted. "Lovely."

"The good news was that I did a lot of good work despite these bosses. I led a team that improved the internship program of one of the organization's business units and assisted them in getting their diversity program off the ground. So when my boss laid me off, one of my supporters in the organization's New York City office hired me as a consultant, which led to the Reverse Mentoring Program a year later."

We continued talking as FIA board members left the restaurant, often stopping by our table to chat. Still holding hands, we strolled back to the hotel thirty minutes later, stopping to pick up my suitcase that I had left earlier at the luggage stand, and requesting a taxi to take me to the airport. We sat together on a bench and continued to talk as the casino cacophony swirled around us. Ten minutes later, we followed a hotel employee to the taxi and hugged each other as the driver put my suitcase into the trunk. The trunk slammed shut.

"Good-bye. Take care," I said. I gave her a lingering kiss, wishing again that we could be more than friends. "But she's married," I reminded myself as I slid into the cab's backseat and closed the door.

After settling into my DC routine with Jules by my side for a couple of weeks, I called Lisa at her office to invite her to take part in a retreat for blind adults I was helping organize. "I'd love to come," she said, "but I will be climbing a mountain in Colorado." She went on to explain that she would be taking part in a program that paired each blind participant with a sighted guide, and that llamas would be carrying their equipment. She seemed pleased to hear from me, so I called her two weeks later. I talked about the retreat and listened as she described her trip: the friends she had made, her sore feet, swimming in a mountain lake, getting caught in a thunderstorm on top of the mountain, and her newfound love of llamas. We enjoyed the conversation so much that I called her the next day. Soon, it became normal for us to talk to each other by phone or e-mail about sports, music, politics, my work, her journey toward her PhD, my job search, her three kids, my guide dogs, her standard poodles, my dad's health, and anything we could think of to keep the conversation going—except her relationship with her husband. Somehow, I just assumed she was happily married, and while her voice still made me horny, I was comfortable maintaining our friendship. I was busy with my professional activities and monitoring Dad's health, and I couldn't imagine moving to an unfamiliar place where I knew no one.

In early September, Lisa interrupted our usual chatter to ask if she could visit me prior to a conference she would be attending in Baltimore. Several weeks later, her friendly greeting warmed my heart as I met her at the elevator. After a brief hug, I walked ahead of her to my apartment.

Lisa stopped short. "What's that disgusting thing hanging on your door that looks like a loaf of chewed-upon bread?"

"Just touch it."

"But it's gross."

"Just touch it."

After a few seconds, I heard the object quietly squeak.

"It's a dog toy!" she said in amused surprise. She squeaked the toy louder, and I heard Jules jump off of the bed and shake himself. While searching for my keys, I explained that the toy helped me be sure that I was standing in front of the right door while serving as a substitute doorbell.

Lisa followed me into my apartment and put her luggage into a corner as Jules pranced around and between our legs. "Hi, Jules, you silly Labrador," she teased, sitting on the sofa and rubbing his head. He jumped onto my bed. "I'm hungry," she announced, so we headed into the kitchen to carry the cheese, crackers, nuts, and white wine I had bought the previous day into the living room. Soon we were sitting side by side on the sofa munching, drinking, and talking as Jules slept on my pillow. I described my experience as a Recording for the Blind's scholarship winner in Washington, DC, and she talked about how during the fall of 2000, her ten-year-old daughter, Ana, and she had taken part in a focus group to help prepare then-presidential candidate Al Gore for his third debate with Governor George W. Bush at Washington University in St. Louis. I talked about how I would be interviewing for a job at an organization in Baltimore.

"That would be a long commute," Lisa pointed out, having just traveled to my apartment from the airport there.

"You're right, but I have dealt with long commutes before. And the job seems a good fit: assisting organizations in becoming more effective in helping immigrants enter the United States."

I told her about my phone interview with my potential boss and wondered aloud if she would pass my "disability test" when we met face-to-face.

Lisa put her wine glass on my desk. "What's that?"

I explained that I had never been offered a job unless the interviewer asked me a question about how I would do the job despite my disability.

"But that's illegal," she protested.

"Actually, it's not. An employer can ask a disability-related question so long as it's also job-related. So someone can ask how I might write a report or conduct research but can't ask about how long I've been blind."

"But aren't employers scared of being sued?"

"Of course, and many are also uncomfortable with the whole concept of blindness."

"So isn't your 'test' a bit unfair?"

"Yes, especially since I don't tell interviewers that I'm blind before I show up. But only those who pass this test have hired me. And those who ask such questions communicate comfort around people of different backgrounds and usually turn out to be good bosses."

The conversation drifted to music, and soon songs of the Dave Matthews Band filled the apartment as Lisa opened a second bottle of wine. Back on the couch, we began talking less with our mouths and more with our lips and hands. Soon the bottle was empty, the stereo system was silent, and we were almost naked.

But she was married, and we were hungry, so we walked to a Cajun restaurant, parking Jules along the way. As we relaxed at an outside table over a third bottle of wine, she began talking about her husband.

I leaned forward. "But you are happily married?"

"No!" she squawked, and described the downward spiral of their relationship with a sadness in her voice that I hadn't heard before. She went on to tell me that she had started divorce proceedings.

"I'm sorry," I stammered as we walked back to my apartment.

"That's okay," she said, perking up. "I should have divorced him years ago."

Well, if she's divorcing her husband …, I thought, buzzed and aroused as we rode the elevator to my apartment.

Her voice bubbled with excitement as she spoke with her three children on her cell phone. "You really love your kids," I said as she snapped her phone shut.

She sat on my twin bed and found my hand. "I do," she gushed, and I lost myself in her voice as she rhapsodized about her kids' strengths.

Talking turned to touching, this time leading to lovemaking. She fell asleep with her head on my chest as Jules slept on the couch.

The next morning, Lisa left for her conference in Baltimore after some hung-over lovemaking and a long shower. I went about my normal life until she called the following afternoon to ask if she could come back to visit for a night after the conference. "Of course," I said, so she arrived the next day. We spent the rest of the afternoon talking, laughing, and cuddling. During the evening, we went to hear my friend Gordon perform at the Banana Café, a funky Mexican restaurant near Union Station, and ended the night with a round of noisy lovemaking.

CHAPTER FOURTEEN:
THE BLESSINGS

SEPTEMBER 2005–JANUARY 2006

Lisa left at 5:30 the next morning to get back to Columbia in time for the Texas-Missouri football game. Four hours later, Jules and I made our weekly trip to the Manhattan Market. After putting the groceries away, I sent Lisa an e-mail telling her how much I had enjoyed our time together. "I don't know what will happen next," I wrote, "but you have opened a door into an unfamiliar, wonderful romantic world that I have heard of and read about but have never really experienced."

"I'm so happy!" Lisa squealed in a voice overflowing with joy at the beginning of a phone call later that evening, "because I feel the same way!"

We continued our separate lives partially connected by phone calls and e-mails. I called her from my apartment and in Wilmington, Delaware, during a meeting of Amtrak's Consumer Advisory Council. She called me from her office. She called me from a Houston Astros-St. Louis Cardinals playoff game. She called me from a U2 concert. And she called me as I hung out with my mom and her two laid-back golden retrievers on Cape Cod.

"Who was that nice girl who called every night?" Mom asked as she drove me to the airport.

"A woman working toward her PhD in engineering," I mumbled.

The Baltimore-based organization offered me a job; again, I was the first blind person they had ever hired. While the two-hour commute made me nervous, the work seemed to be interesting and a good fit with my skills. The salary was reasonable, and they would allow me to work from home twice a week. "My boss's family raised a puppy for a guide dog school in California while she was in high school," I told Lisa during one of our phone conversations, "and she passed my disability test by asking how I could pick up on those subtle visual cues that hint at what's going on behind what's being said while working with groups."

"What did you say?"

"That subtleties, like the tone and speed of voices, the clearing of throats, yawns, drumming fingers and feet, tapping pencils, and rustling chairs, often mirror visual cues."

"But aren't there things you miss?"

"Of course. But sighted people miss cues too. And several of my colleagues have told me that they misread some of the signals they can see."

Three days before my start date, I attended my last meeting at the large NGO. I had spent my first four months there conducting interviews, reviewing documents, and preparing a draft of a $15 million strategic plan aimed at improving the way the organization served its disabled employees and customers. After numerous rewrites, the head of the organization had approved the plan, and I spent the next eighteen months conducting workshops, evaluating training materials, leading focus groups, and providing input on human resources–related policies. Now Jules and I would be observing a presentation detailing progress toward plan goals to another senior official. After several remarks from team leaders, the official gave his approval and started strolling around the table, making small talk and shaking hands. "I know I'm not supposed to pat your service animal," he proclaimed as he shook my hand, "but I'm going to anyway."

"How rude!" exclaimed one of my colleagues as she assisted Jules and me through the winding corridors to the street.

"He wasn't as obnoxious as a certain former New York City mayor," I said, and told her about how my third dog, Dunbar, and I had been attending a reception in the ballroom of a Manhattan hotel that Guiding Eyes had organized to honor the mayor's support of the school. "I was standing in a corner with several people, and I heard his voice coming closer and closer, finally stopping right next to me. Dunbar's tags rattled as the voice continued, and when I reached down to investigate, I grazed another hand on his head. The hand jerked away toward the voice, which continued to drone on as if nothing had happened."

My colleague gasped. "He didn't apologize?"

"No. He never even introduced himself!"

At 6:30 a.m. on the last Monday in October, Jules and I strode to the Woodley Park Metro station to begin our first commute to the new job. The Metro took us to Union Station, where we boarded a commuter train, which rattled and wheezed its way to the Camden Yards station. A hoarse, cheery voice belonging to Sarah greeted us as we got off. She lived nearby and had volunteered to walk with us from the station to the office for the first several days so that Jules and I could cement the route that a specially trained mobility instructor had taught us a week earlier into our memories. Over the next several weeks, she introduced me to office staff and many of the leaders of the organizations I would be working with. She e-mailed materials for me to review so I could begin to understand the challenges faced by immigrants and those who serve them. She worked with me to figure out how to complete my time sheets and other paperwork.

But first I had to join a small group of fellow employees in an airy carpeted room where we listened to several managers chirp about the organization's glorious history. "At least it only lasted four hours instead of seven days at that government agency and three at that stodgy bank on Wall Street," I grumbled to Lisa during a phone call later that evening. "And they did give us locally baked pastries."

During the rest of the week, I filled out forms in the human resources office, took part in a lunch with my boss and the rest of the work team, began learning about office procedures, and worked with their computer expert so I could access their computer system using JAWS. On Friday morning, I attended my first weekly staff meeting, where I fell asleep in the middle of a video presentation.

"Not good," Lisa said during another phone conversation.

"No," I agreed. "I'm still adjusting to the two-hour commute. And I have always had trouble staying awake during videos because I dislike movies despite my mom's insistence that I learn to enjoy them."

"Maybe it was *because* of her insistence?"

"Perhaps. She made heroic efforts to connect me with the sighted world, but I just can't, or won't, get excited about movies and TV shows."

After nearly falling asleep during another staff meeting, I started trying to figure out how others were staying awake, and began hearing stifled yawns, rustling newspapers, whispered comments about knitting patterns, and snorts from colleagues. So instead of focusing on the meeting with my hands in my lap, I began reading a book, which kept me awake while earning me praise from colleagues who thought I was reviewing meeting-related materials instead of reading about young wizards, courageous spies, or self-righteous politicians. Several months later, the leadership team got the message and canceled the meetings.

My work was far more interesting: organizing a retreat scheduled to take place in early March for executive directors of nineteen nonprofit organizations around the country; coaching managers concerning issues related to strategic planning, motivating employees, and board development; organizing workshops for office staff; and leading a grant review process that determined how to divide $250,000 among twenty-five organizations. I also interviewed my fellow employees to learn about their work and beliefs concerning the purpose of the six-member team to which I belonged. According to the information on the organization's internal website, our mission was to "increase the capacities" of employees, but what did that mean? No one seemed to know.

"What training would help you do a better job?" I asked.

"I don't know," people would mumble with a tinge of irritation.

I soon realized that they had good reason to be annoyed. Since they enjoyed their work and did it well, a capacity-building team seemed superfluous and offensive as our skills were about the same as those of our colleagues. So why was the team created? Again, most didn't know, but several employees told me of a rumor that it was formed during a round of layoffs so that they wouldn't have to fire my boss. They also told me that I was the third person in two years she had hired to fill the position I now held, and that if she started nitpicking somebody's work or questioning their motives, she was getting ready to fire them. "And there's nothing you can do because she's too well-connected," they warned.

~

A MONTH AFTER MY START date, Lisa visited me for several days and was already in my apartment when Jules and I arrived from work. He started sniffing enthusiastically under the door as I took my keys out of my pocket.

"Are you happy Lisa's here?" I asked him.

He sneezed while wagging his tail and sprinted across the apartment after I had unlocked the door. Lisa greeted him in a muffled voice from the bed as I put the harness, leash, and backpack on the closet shelf. I walked over to the voice. "Hey, Lisa, how are you?" I searched for a hand to hold or lips to kiss but found that she was totally covered in blankets.

"I'm freezing," she complained, uncovering her head.

"I'm hot," I said after emerging from a passionate kiss.

After some joint energetic fun in bed, she emerged from her cocoon, and we began our journey together as a couple. We shopped for groceries. She cooked using the stove and oven that I hadn't touched for eight years. We visited the Banana Café to hear Gordon perform. We wandered around the neighborhood enjoying the clear, breezy weather. Lisa met some of my friends at one of the boys'-night-out get-togethers. And we began learning to muddle through the inevitable conflicts that all couples face: the temperature of the room, who would be responsible for what, and how to best support each other.

Lisa returned to Columbia the Tuesday before Thanksgiving to be with her family, leaving behind some home-cooked food. On Thanksgiving night, I called to tell her that this food had been especially meaningful because I had spent the day alone instead of celebrating with my stepmother, Pat, and my dad. She talked about how hard it was for her to be thankful while being around the man she was in the process of divorcing.

180

During her next visit two weeks later, we enjoyed a leisurely dinner at a local seafood restaurant, where she tried to explain her research. While I didn't fully understand her work, I was impressed with her shift from bubbly girl to sophisticated scientist. The following evening, we attended a rowdy Christmas party and kissed and groped each other during the half-hour return trip on the Metro as Jules slept under my feet. We woke up late the following morning, and after luxuriating in each other's company, I told her that I needed to finish a project. I turned on my computer, put my headphones on, and started working.

"Did you know that the music's coming through your speakers?" Lisa called several minutes later from the bathroom.

"No," I said, annoyed with myself as the "project" was supposed to be a surprise. I finished my work and sat next to her on the couch.

"I was planning to give you a CD of my favorite Christmas carols," I began, "but the surprise is gone."

She found my hand and told me not to worry.

"Actually," I continued more nervously, "these are my favorite arrangements of Christmas carols that I have written."

"What?" She seemed more confused.

After several more stuttering starts, I realized that she needed to hear the full story. So I told her about my relationship with music growing up. I told her of my failed efforts to enter the popular music industry, and of my decision to leave music behind when I started my first full-time job.

But I hadn't abandoned music. During the next twenty years, I had written several pieces for the hand-bell choir that my mom directed, several of which had been performed at regional hand-bell conferences and one of which had been published by a small publisher in Connecticut. I had also written several choral arrangements that the Friends-in-Art chorus had performed during showcases at several ACB conventions. "And every year since 1984," I told her, "I have written three funky four-part vocal arrangements of Christmas carols. I recorded them using a four-track cassette recorder, mixed them onto cassettes, and used them as Christmas cards."

"What a great idea!"

"And then a couple of years ago, Gordon installed MIDI software on my new computer, and my Christmas carol arrangements featured instrumental sounds generated from a keyboard synthesizer I had recently bought. You were listening to one of those arrangements when I forgot to turn off my amplifier."

"Wow!"

"And then last year I got the idea of composing new melodies for carol texts instead of just arranging the more familiar tunes."

"What do you mean?"

"You know the carol 'We Three Kings of Orient Are?'" I sang a couple of phrases of the solemn, melancholy waltz. Lisa hummed along. "I created a different melody that's more bouncy and joyful. Do you want to hear it?" She squeezed my hand, so I clicked on the carol and rejoined her on the couch as six voices and a synthesized harp filled the apartment.

"That was awesome!" she said when the tune ended. "Who sang the vocals?"

"I did."

"Really! How?"

I explained that I would sing the melody on one track and then record the other parts while listening to the melody. "Would you like to hear more?" I asked.

"Yes!"

During the next twenty minutes, I played some of my arrangements: "How Brightly Shines the Morning Star" for brass and timpani; "Santa Claus Is Coming to Town" for string quartet; "Jingle Bell Rock" arranged in the style of a Tchaikovsky waltz; "Holly Jolly Christmas" for brass band; "White Christmas" with a reggae feel; "Lo How a Rose E'er Blooming" for brass quintet; "Frosty the Snowman" arranged as a late 1950s rock tune; "Good King Wenceslas" for percussion ensemble; "Oh Christmas Tree" for marching band; and "We Wish You a Merry Christmas" for steel drum band. Sudden silence fell as the last note died away.

"Are you all right?" I asked, sitting down and putting my arm around her.

"I'm overwhelmed," Lisa half-whispered, putting her arm around me. "You're amazing."

As we sat silently on my threadbare couch with our arms around each other, I felt wrapped in waves of peaceful joy. I couldn't believe that such a talented caring woman would not just admire my accomplishments but love me for who I was and who I might become. And I wanted to protect her from all the evil people in the world even though I knew I couldn't. I wanted to be there for her as she struggled to escape from a husband who had been nasty to her during surgeries on her eyes, back, and ankle, while gloating about sleeping with one of her best friends for the past year. I wanted to encourage her as she tried to balance roles of PhD candidate and parent. For the first time, I really thought about what it might be like to move from a settled, secure space to unfamiliar surroundings where I would be responsible for supporting three kids I hadn't even met. Could I do it? Should I do it? All I knew was that she had given me the chance to explore love's wonderful possibilities, and I wanted to continue the journey.

"I love you," I whispered in her ear.

"I love you too, baby," she murmured.

Lisa returned to Columbia the following afternoon with a CD of my greatest hits. After hugging our good-byes outside Woodley Park's fare gate, Jules and I returned home and called Mom. "Are you sitting down?" I asked.

"Why?"

"I think I'm in love."

"Wow! I don't think I've ever heard you say that."

"You're right; I haven't."

"So who's the girl?"

"Remember the woman working toward her PhD in engineering who called every night during my last visit?"

"Of course. I knew you weren't telling me everything."

A few days before Christmas, Mom called to tell me that she was planning to go to New York City on New Year's Eve to visit my dad for the first time since their divorce, and that my sister, Jenny, would be coming from Colorado to join her, and that it would be nice if we could come as well. Later that evening, I told Lisa about the "invitation."

"Sounds like a command performance to me," she observed.

"Probably." I laughed. "But I'll still love you if you don't come."

She thought about it for a moment. "Let's do it."

So we found a room at a Manhattan hotel that was empty on New Year's Eve. We booked the needed Amtrak and airline seats. Lisa was able to find someone to look after her kids as her husband wasn't available. We made arrangements to hang out with Mitch and Donna, the couple who had brought us together in Birmingham, Alabama.

Yet we almost didn't make the trip. I had spent Christmas alone in my DC apartment while Lisa had forced herself to be cheerful around her husband for the sake of her kids. During an e-mail exchange, I alluded to my stepmother Pat's warm relationship with a friend who assumed she was my girlfriend. She had recently called Lisa my guide dog and had asked weird questions about our sex lives. Much to my annoyance, Lisa wanted to know if I still was in love with her, and I wondered if we were ready for the meet-the-parents trip. Lisa called the night before she was scheduled to arrive, and we spoke about our miserable Christmases and how it was sometimes easier for each of us to pull into our shells instead of reaching out for emotional support. After two days together, we regained our mojo and rang the doorbell of Dad's apartment on the afternoon of New year's Eve.

"The door's open! Come in!" Mom and Jenny called.

"Happy, be quiet!" Pamela, the live-in housekeeper, snapped, trying to stop the toy poodle's incessant yapping.

We entered into a noisy muddle of hugs, handshakes, babbled introductions, Labrador snorts, and Happy barks.

"Where's Dad?" I asked, wondering why I hadn't heard his voice.

"Dr. Altschul fell down and bumped his head," Pamela said. "He's fine, but he's at the emergency room just in case."

The confused melee continued as we sorted out drink and snack preferences and who should sit where. Several hours later, Happy's high-pitched yaps interrupted our friendly wine-fueled conversation to announce Dad's arrival. "I'm hungry," he groused in response to our cheery greetings.

"The food's on its way, Dr. Altschul," Pamela called from the kitchen as Happy grumbled in her arms.

But even when the food arrived, Dad didn't take part in the friendly banter, barely responding to Lisa's efforts to talk to him.

"But he couldn't keep his eyes off of me," she said as we walked to a nearby subway station with a mixture of light sleet and snow blowing into our faces. We had said our good-byes, promising to return the following afternoon. "He was watching me while eating, and the spaghetti was flying everywhere: in his mouth, on his clothes, and on the floor."

Later, as we emerged from a station near the hotel where we would be staying, she observed that the subway reeked of urine, and that the Metro was much nicer.

"You're right," I told her, "but you can get to more places using the subway."

We left the hotel around noon on New Year's Day to meet up with Mitch and Donna, who had flown in from California to visit friends thirty blocks north of us. Holding hands, we strolled uptown as I described how I had prowled the area with Heidi the Weimaraner to make connections with "jingle houses" and song publishers when I was trying to break into the music business. I told her about how I would work both Nan the chocolate Lab and my third dog, Dunbar, the two-mile route from Penn Station to my apartment every day during the height of the Manhattan afternoon rush hour. Lisa marveled at the massive cleanup taking place in Times Square after the festivities the night before and commented on the buildings we passed and people who milled around us.

After joining Mitch and Donna at a mediocre Puerto Rican restaurant, we took a cab to Dad's apartment. Jules settled into a corner of the living room as we chatted with Jenny, while Mom and Dad talked in another room. We all came together to continue yesterday's cheerful banter while gorging on take-out Chinese food. "You must come with us to France in May for my sister Connie's eightieth birthday party," Mom told Lisa as we said our good-byes.

"You should come to France if you can," I told her the following afternoon as we rode an Amtrak train back to my DC apartment. "Everybody loves Aunt Connie." I told Lisa that she always cheered the loudest after my musical performances. I talked about how much I had enjoyed my ten-day family reunion that she had hosted in Roscoff, a small fishing village near the English Channel when I was seventeen: how family members cheered me on as I explored several pipe organs in large cathedrals and small churches that were built in the seventeenth and eighteenth centuries; the bumpy rides on the backs of mopeds and tandem bicycles to sidewalk cafés to drink wine and eat crepes; the swims in an icy salt-water pool; the fresh seafood, artichokes, and pastries; the seagulls that had squawked Jenny and me awake at seven o'clock every morning; and the exuberant conversations that had switched seamlessly between French and English.

Back in my apartment, Lisa and I started listening to the college football championship game between the Texas Longhorns and the University of Southern California Trojans, resolving not to make love until halftime. We failed spectacularly.

"You know that Pat and I hoped you would make passionate love with someone in our bed while you were alone in our apartment?" my dad asked a couple of weeks later. Lisa was back in Missouri, and I was visiting him in Manhattan prior to beginning my last year running the Reverse Mentoring Program for that London-based corporation.

"No!" I had nearly shouted, astounded that he would say such a thing, as the only time I remember us talking about sex was when Mom had forced him to tell me about wet dreams when I was ten.

"Well, we did," he declared. "And we always wondered if it had happened when we found our bed more rumpled than usual."

"I'm sorry to disappoint you," I said, trying not to laugh, "but it didn't happen."

We spoke about my relationships with women living in Brooklyn, Texas, and Greenwich Village, and of Pat's failed efforts as matchmaker.

"But what about Lisa?" I asked. Dad was silent. "Do you want me to be with Lisa or one of my other women friends you've met?"

"Lee-sah," he answered huskily.

Perhaps moving to Columbia is not so crazy after all, I thought as Jules and I weaved through the Manhattan crowds to Penn Station.

CHAPTER FIFTEEN: CONTROL

FEBRUARY–MAY 2006

I was edgy at the beginning of Lisa's next visit in early February, having just returned to a drizzly DC day from a four-day business trip to Arizona. I had to leave Jules with Gifford at the Walters because of my boss's concern that the guards at a detention center we would be visiting might balk at allowing him to enter the facility. While this would likely have been illegal, I have learned over the years that some battles just aren't worth fighting, especially since my boss and I weren't getting along.

Lisa's joyful spirit kept my edginess at bay until my warbling phone jarred me awake at nine o'clock the following morning. The brittle tinny voice of my boss echoing through her speaker phone chirped a greeting. She told me that Sarah was with her.

"Hi, Sarah," I interrupted.

"Hey, Peter," she mumbled in a flat let's-just-get-through-this voice.

"Who is it?" Lisa mumbled.

I turned away from the phone. "My boss. I'm sorry."

For the next twenty minutes, my boss droned on about the list of tasks she had created, how each task should be completed, and who would be responsible for what. Sarah and I made the necessary agreement noises, knowing that we would figure out how to get the work done when she wasn't around.

"That sounded like fun," Lisa said when I hung up the phone.

"I'm sorry," I mumbled. "But it's really annoying," I fumed. "Sarah and I didn't want her to come with us because we were irritated with her micromanaging our work. Then she tells us at the last minute that she's coming. And now she's still trying to tell us how to do our jobs."

"Come back to bed," Lisa coaxed.

"I can't. I have too much work."

I began plowing through e-mails as Lisa slept.

"It's a beautiful day," Lisa said as we came back from brunch. "Let's hang out at the park."

"I can't. I have too much work," I snapped.

I continued working, but the brooding silence surrounding Lisa became too distracting.

"I'm sorry," I said, joining her on the sofa. "It *is* a nice day. Let's go for a walk."

"But then we won't be here when Jules shows up."

Linda arrived with Jules and Gifford thirty minutes later. As the women made greeting noises, Jules sauntered around the apartment and slithered between my legs as Gifford shredded one of his toys. Lisa observed that Gifford was a short, stocky curly fireplug that rooted around like a pig. "That's not nice," Linda complained, laughing.

After the dogs calmed down, Linda, Lisa, and I walked to a café across the street to continue our conversation. I have never liked coffee ever since gagging on my first sip when I was eight years old, but Lisa loved vanilla lattés and had been encouraging me to try them. After settling in around a table, I told her that I thought I might want to try a coffee drink, hoping to get back in her good graces. "Really," she said, and ordered me a large, frothy, chocolate coffee concoction.

"You finished it!" Lisa exclaimed as we prepared to leave. "How was it?"

"Not bad," I hedged.

After saying good-bye to Linda and Gifford, I called Mom, thinking that Lisa might talk to her as well, but forgot to tell her. "I'm going for a walk," she announced in a huff, slamming the door behind her. During dinner at the Cajun restaurant where we had eaten during our first night alone, she was unhappy because I didn't give her a piece of the tuna steak I had promised to save for her. "You need to treat me better," she snapped several hours later after we had made love with a Cheryl Crowe CD playing in the background. I apologized, and soon she was asleep with her head on my chest.

But I couldn't sleep, which didn't surprise me because I usually would lie awake beating myself up after failing at something. But this time I was flying, exuberant, immortal. I was certain that our relationship couldn't fail. And I still couldn't sleep, so I got out of bed, turned on my computer, and continued attacking my e-mails.

"What *are* you doing?" Lisa asked an hour later. "You woke me up."

"But my headphones are on."

"You're pounding the keys."

"I'm sorry," I mumbled, and then the same thought hit us: *it's the coffee.*

"Come back to bed," she coaxed, and this time I listened.

We emerged at three o'clock the following afternoon, and holding hands, strolled to a local Asian restaurant, parking Jules along the way. Over lunch, I told her about my Arizona business trip. On the morning of our first day there, we had toured a detention center where immigrants who couldn't prove that they were here legally were held. Loud voices and doors clanging shut assailed us as we walked through the narrow halls that reeked of chemicals. We had also observed the assembly-line court proceedings where a bored Anglo male judge's voice had ordered the deportation of a stream of immigrants with Hispanic last names. Sarah, my boss, and I had each commented about the unpleasantness of the place as the three of us and our tour guide settled in for lunch on the patio of a Florence, Arizona, restaurant.

After a waitress had served us cold drinks, our tour guide, an immigration attorney and the executive director of a small nonprofit that our organization supported, began a well-practiced rant about the harsh conditions of the detention center. I interrupted to ask if most of the people there were here illegally. "Yes," she had said, but added that some were innocent either because they were married to someone who was here legally or because they were fleeing domestic violence or political persecution. She went on to explain that the statutes were convoluted and that there weren't enough immigration attorneys willing to help people with little money. She reminded us that it could take up to eighteen months to get in front of a judge, and that the detained were stuck behind bars until their cases were decided.

I told Lisa that after lunch, our boss had talked nonstop as we toured the small, dingy office of the executive director. "Why didn't you talk more?" she had groused during our trip back to the hotel. I kept my mouth shut. "Don't worry about it," Sarah had said later. "She's just being herself."

The following day, we had visited the larger more comfortable office of another client, and while my boss seemed happier, I noticed that she had encouraged the executive director to contact others within our organization with problems that I had been hired to address.

$\sim$

LISA AND I NEXT CAME together during a weekend in late February in Ventura Beach, California, where she was attending a prestigious conference for biomedical engineers. "I hope you don't mind," she said as the three of us walked on a nearby beach late on a Friday evening, "but I have to attend sessions during the next couple of mornings."

"Don't worry," I assured her. "I'll either sleep or review grant proposals."

But instead of attending to our work, we cocooned together in our hotel room or at the beach with the waves lapping at our feet. We had lunch with my favorite cousin, Hale, a retired management consultant who lived nearby. We visited a local Walgreens, where Lisa bought supplies for a presentation she would be making. She described her frustration with her husband's broken promises and surly attitude, and I worried aloud about my deteriorating relationship with my boss and my dad's health.

And we dreamed together about what life might be like when I joined her in Missouri.

Sarah met me at the airport in Portland, Oregon, on Sunday evening, and we drove through a howling rainstorm to the austere but comfortable lodge where the retreat for nineteen executive directors that I had been organizing for months would take place. During the following evening's reception, participants spoke quietly while my boss chirped continuously. The workshops started the following morning. After I encouraged participants to talk with each other about the health of their organizations, they spent the next day and a half teaching each other about fundraising, media relations, the effective use of technology, and motivating staff.

"You're not doing enough," my boss snapped as she walked with Sarah, Jules, and me to the last breakfast of the retreat.

I protested that the high quality of the discussions during the workshops and the excited chatter during breaks told me that participants were both learning from and enjoying their time together.

"Don't worry," Sarah told me as our boss stalked off. "She doesn't know what she's talking about."

During the wrap-up discussion, participants talked about how the retreat was the best they had ever attended, described how they would run their organizations differently because of what they had learned, and came up with ways they could work together better.

"My boss wasn't pleased," I told Lisa the next day on my cell phone as I waited to change planes. "While driving me to the airport, she listed my faults as an employee: that I had fallen asleep during a meeting, that she had overheard me getting the name of the organization slightly wrong, and how I was too disengaged."

"Did she ever mention any of this prior to the retreat?" Lisa asked.

"No! And it was bizarre that she would talk about my shortcomings immediately after what was a successful retreat."

"Perhaps you should have been more involved?"

"It would have been better if I hadn't briefly fallen asleep during one of the workshops," I admitted, "but it was because I allowed the participants to control how they were learning that made the retreat work so well."

Late on the following Monday afternoon, my boss called me into her office to tell me that she was putting me on probation for three months. *It's over,* I thought to myself, remembering the warnings of my colleagues about her pattern of nitpicking the work of those she wanted to fire. I knew that being put on probation would make it harder to find another job, and that I would be leaving anyway in order to join Lisa in Missouri. But I was angry with the unfairness of her decision and wanted to support retreat participants to make the changes that they had committed to making and work on other projects I had been assigned. I asked for some time to think.

I stalled, vaguely hoping that she would change her mind, as I had heard rumors that she might be promoted. After delaying for as long as I dared, I sent her an e-mail in mid-April stating that I wanted to resign but would be willing to stay through Labor Day.

My relationship with Lisa suddenly began unraveling in mid-April when I brusquely announced during her next visit that I had no interest in strolling through the display of cherry blossoms, a highlight of the DC spring. The unraveling spun out of control when despite her best efforts, I didn't understand the financial sacrifices she was making in order to pay for her airfare, and then couldn't accept that this sacrifice was causing her such emotional pain. "I'll talk to you tomorrow night," she snapped, putting an end to a frustratingly futile circular conversation.

But she didn't call the following evening … or the evening after that.

I sent her several apologetic e-mails that I hoped would comfort her, but her prickly responses made it clear that I was failing. After yet another prickly response, I sat dejectedly at my desk, barely registering the sports radio talk show humming in the background and not knowing where Jules was sleeping. "It's over," I said to myself, sensing that I had failed her in a powerful way. I didn't want to hurt her anymore. So I slowly crafted an e-mail expressing my sadness and suggesting how our relationship could end as gracefully as possible. I painstakingly checked the e-mail to be sure it was as perfect as it could be. I rechecked my work, not wanting to send the e-mail but knowing that I must …

And then the phone warbled. It was Lisa. We spoke haltingly and carefully about how much we had unintentionally hurt each other, and we decided to try to pick up the pieces. "You're a pain in the ass," she e-mailed me later that evening, "but I love you anyway." And as we began restoring our relationship over the next month, I came to understand that my emotional steadiness complemented her more deeply experienced feelings, and that I needed to give her the support and space she needed to work through those feelings so she could harness their energy to move her forward.

Lisa and I had talked excitedly about our upcoming trip to Roscoff, France, with my family to celebrate Aunt Connie's eightieth birthday since our New Year's Eve trip to Manhattan. She had even agreed to play Aunt Connie in a skit honoring her quirks, even though she had never acted before. "But you have stage presence," I told her, reminding her of the piano recitals she had performed in as a kid and the horses she had shown throughout Missouri and Iowa as a young adult.

Two weeks before we left, I took part in a conference call with my dad and his doctor. As Dad coughed in the background, the doctor told us that his melanoma had spread and that his chances of recovery weren't good.

"What are the options?" I asked.

"We can try a more aggressive form of treatment," she said, "or we can control his pain and arrange for hospice services."

"How long might he live without treatment?"

"Hard to tell, but my best guess is six months to a year." She paused. "So what would you like to do, Dr. Altschul?"

Dad was silent.

"You don't have to decide right now," she told him.

He remained silent.

"Dad," I said hesitantly, "you have always said that you didn't want any heroic actions done on your behalf." I paused. "I will support whatever you decide, but—"

Dad grunted something.

"What was that?" the doctor asked.

"I don't want anything done for me," he slurred.

"That's fine," she said. "If you're sure, I'll begin the process of connecting you to a hospice."

"I'm sure," he grunted with a trace of his old impatience.

"I'm proud of you, Dad," I told him.

"Why are you proud of him?" Lisa asked later.

"Because he stuck to his beliefs under stress. I'm not sure I could do that."

~

LISA AND I FLEW TO Paris with my mom, my favorite cousin, Hale, and his wife, Sue, and Aunt Sibyl, the wife of my favorite uncle, leaving Jules to hang out with Gifford at the Walters. We settled into a drafty room at Aunt Connie's rambling, vibrant house, and explored the narrow winding streets of the village and the beach. Lisa's voice bubbled with excitement and awe as she marveled at the fishing boats, the Brittany Renaissance architecture, the ancient churches, and quaint shops we walked by as cars and mopeds zoomed around us on the cobblestone streets and gulls squawked overhead. My family marveled at her ability to talk science with the director of an oceanographic research center. In the mornings, we feasted on homegrown strawberries and fresh pastries, and devoured crepes, seafood, and fresh vegetables, washing it down with local wines and hard ciders during the afternoons and evenings. We spent three days exploring the local countryside with Hale and Sue, spending two nights at a bed and breakfast attached to a family dairy farm.

A large crowd of family and local dignitaries came to celebrate Aunt Connie's eightieth birthday. The skit starring Lisa took place late in the evening in front of tables littered with empty wine bottles and the carcasses of lobsters, crabs, and shellfish. After her bravura performance, I sat in a corner as she worked the room absorbing congratulatory hugs and kisses.

"What a good sport," Mom said.

"Absolutely *charmante*," proclaimed Aunt Connie after she stopped laughing.

During the flight home, Lisa and I hugged and held hands as we dreamed about our life together in Columbia, Missouri: the kind of house we wanted, the best way for me to find a job, how I could begin to be a part of her kids' lives, and the fun we would have together. But when should I make my first visit? Before or after the upcoming ACB convention in early July? We finally decided I should make two visits: one before and one after the convention. I wasn't sure I could leap into this new life, but I loved her enough to give it my best shot.

CHAPTER SIXTEEN: LOOSENING TIES

JUNE–SEPTEMBER 2006

On a hot, still day in late June, Lisa, her fifteen-year-old daughter, Ana, and Luke, their four-year-old standard poodle, were in their driveway to welcome Jules and me to Columbia for the first time. Luke growled as we stepped out of the van that we had ridden in from the St. Louis airport. Lisa had told me about how he sailed over six-foot fences to terrorize cats and patrol the neighborhood, and how he swiped food from kitchen counters. I didn't quite believe her because of my stepmother's pampered toy poodle. I believed her now.

"Hi Luke, you vicious dog," I called. He growled more loudly as Jules stood by my side gently wagging his tail.

"Hi, honey," Lisa called from across the driveway. "Shut up, Luke," she ordered. He ignored her.

Ana observed that Jules was the first dog Luke hadn't intimidated, and I said that I wasn't surprised because he had irritated my boss by not submitting to her dog's I'm-in-charge posturing.

"Perhaps she didn't like you because you refused to bow down to her," Lisa suggested.

"Too late now. She hired my replacement ten days ago; she couldn't wait to get rid of me."

"It is kind of sad, though," I said as we walked into the house, "because she told me during our last one-on-one meeting that she had hoped that I could repair her relationships for her. Of course no one can repair another person's relationships. And it reminded me of a former boss who was having an affair with someone in the office telling me that my job was to make him look good. 'No, it's not,' I had snapped. 'My job is to make the organization look good.' I knew I couldn't say something similar to my boss, so I made soft apologetic sounds and left as quickly as possible."

(Sarah told me six months later that our boss had been promoted and that the person she hired to replace her had pounded his fists on the table during staff meetings and hated women. Another employee had seen him watching S and M videos starring himself wearing an orange speedo.)

After stowing Luke and my luggage in the house, Ana drove us to a Japanese restaurant where they told me about Luke's harassment of Tiger, the family cat. I told them about Marmalade, an orange cat that we had bought for Jenny's seventeenth birthday. He had purred when I carried him around the house even though I accidentally shut him up in my shirt drawer and sat on him every Wednesday night after choir practice.

"Awwww, poor kitty," Ana groaned.

I told them that our friendship had ended when Heidi the Weimaraner had cornered Marmalade during her first visit to Cape Cod. Mom had intervened to prevent further damage, but he had hidden in a wicker basket six feet off of the floor in her bedroom during future visits, and whenever I walked in, she would describe the "I hate you" glare he had given me.

"Awwww, poor kitty," Ana repeated.

"Over time, though, Marmalade could sneak through the house without Heidi glaring at him," I continued, "and the people who looked after her when she retired told me that she would cuddle with their cat and that she had tried to pee in its litter box."

"Awwww, how sweet," Ana said.

Back at the house, we chatted until Ana's two brothers came home from summer school.

"Mom, when can we buy fireworks?" piped eight-year-old Louis from the door. He and his nine-year-old brother, Joseph, launched into a spirited discussion about the bottle rockets, mortars, and other explosives they were planning to set off on July Fourth.

"What's wrong?" Lisa asked me.

"Nothing. But isn't it illegal for the boys to shoot fireworks?"

Everybody assured me that it was not only legal but expected that everyone explode things while eating barbecue and drinking beer on the Fourth.

"Don't you want to say hi to the guest?" Lisa asked.

"Hi, Peter," they said before hurrying away.

During dinner, Joseph rhapsodized about his model airplane collection and his pet python named Monty. We talked about our trip that we would be making the following day to Lisa's timeshare near Branson, Missouri. During dessert, I presented gifts: a container of fair-trade chocolate and individual cards, each containing the braille alphabet and their names in braille. Over hot chocolate, the kitchen became still as I told them about the braille cell containing six dots in two rows of three, and how these dots are combined to form letters, numbers, and music notation. I showed them how the six keys on my Braille Lite corresponded to each dot of the braille cell.

"Isn't that interesting?" Lisa asked the boys. "Thank him for the gifts, and it's bedtime."

"Thank you," they mumbled.

"Good night," I said as they disappeared into their rooms.

The next day, Joseph, Louis, Jules, and I piled into the back of a van, along with luggage, boxes, and a cooler full of food for the four-hour trip to the timeshare, leaving Luke behind with a neighbor. With Lisa's guidance from the passenger seat, Ana drove, stopping for coffee, bathroom breaks, and lunch at Lamberts, a restaurant that serves large amounts of greasy Southern food and "thrown rolls," which servers hurl at customers. "Heads up," one called, throwing a roll in our direction. Jules leapt into the air and swallowed it whole. The boys cheered as many around us laughed.

"Very nice," I told him. "Now lie down."

At the timeshare, Lisa and Ana unpacked as Louis dragged me around the cabin describing the animal heads mounted on the walls. During the next three days, I tried to make friends with the kids as we swam, paddled around aimlessly in canoes, threw pillows at each other, thwarted attacks from pirates and skunks, played cards, and rode roller coasters at a local amusement park.

We were exhausted when we returned to Columbia, but we had to buy fireworks and food for the July Fourth festivities. On the afternoon of the Fourth, the boys started shooting off fireworks with other neighborhood kids until one o'clock the following morning, stopping to inhale ribs, potato salad, watermelon, cake, and soda. Lisa and I had drinks with one of Columbia's most respected attorneys, who cross-examined me about my future plans. Jules and I returned to my DC apartment late in the afternoon of July fifth and slept throughout much of the following day.

Three days later, Lisa and I came together in Jacksonville, Florida, at the ACB convention, where we agreed that my visit had gone well. Then came the whirlwind of activities. We attended the Guiding Eyes reception, where I introduced her as a friend.

"She looks like more than a friend to me!" exclaimed one of the instructors who had supported my learning to work with my third dog, Dunbar.

I applauded as Lisa received another ACB scholarship toward her PhD work. "That was amazing," Lisa told me after she observed my efforts to prepare the Friends-in-Art chorus to sing my setting of the "We Three Kings" text that she had heard the previous December. I thanked her and suggested that she might want to come to the FIA suite the following morning because I would be rehearsing a song that I would be dedicating to her at the showcase. The following morning, I started practicing the Stephen Sondheim song "Not While I'm Around" with Janiece accompanying on the piano.

"Not bad," I said after the second run-through, and we began discussing small errors that we hoped we would correct before the performance the following evening.

Lisa put her arms around me. "That was beautiful," she sobbed into my shoulder.

I thanked her while focusing on Janiece.

"That was so beautiful," Lisa repeated, sobbing harder as Janiece continued talking.

"I'm sorry," I interrupted, "but my woman is sobbing in my arms."

Janiece stopped short. "I'm sorry. I didn't know."

Lisa laughed through her tears. "That's okay," we said, lurching from the suite with our arms around each other.

~

BACK IN DC, I CALLED Lisa late on the following Sunday morning. We were talking about the convention when my phone beeped. It was Pamela, Dad and Pat's live-in housekeeper. "Peter," she said in a hushed voice, "I think Dr. Altschul's gone."

"Are you sure?"

"I think he's stopped breathing."

I told her to call 911 and to keep me posted. I clicked back to Lisa. "That was Pamela," I said numbly, "I think Dad's dead."

"I'm sorry," she said softly.

"It's okay," I said, searching for something to say. "He built a good life for himself after his family was forced to leave Germany in the 1930s."

"But weren't they Lutheran?"

"Yes, but the Nazis decreed that they had too much Jewish blood. So he arrived here with no money but with a full scholarship from 'a small place called Harvard.'"

"A small place called Harvard," Lisa repeated, amused.

"That's right." I smiled. "He had never heard of the place until he arrived. But he received his PhD at twenty-two. He tried to enlist in the army, but they turned him down because they thought he might be a spy. After World War II, he began a long successful teaching career, first at Bryn Mawr and then at Sarah Lawrence College, where he married two of his students."

"What a life."

"I think he lived and died the way he wanted."

My phone beeped again. The caller identified himself as a police officer who confirmed that Dad was dead and asked if I thought there was any foul play involved. When I assured him that there wasn't, he told me that the body would be moved to a morgue and could be picked up at our convenience. I thanked him and passed the news on to Lisa.

"I'm so sorry," she repeated.

"Me too," I said sadly, "but at least he died at home with dignity."

"What about the funeral?"

"I hope to keep it simple; he hated ceremonies."

"Let me know when you have a date."

"You don't have to come."

"But I want to be with you."

At six o'clock on a rancid, humid Manhattan evening ten days later, shrill yaps from Happy the toy poodle announced the arrival of those who would be participating in the ceremony honoring Dad. Lisa, Jenny, Pamela, Jules, and I mingled with representatives from Sarah Lawrence College and his friends from Manhattan and Trenton. We ate food from a local German deli while music of Mozart, his favorite composer, played in the background. After about thirty minutes, Jenny and I asked guests to sit anywhere they wished and began reading a tribute we had written for his eighty-fifth birthday.

"Hi, Dad," I read from my Braille Lite as Jules lay by my side, "we want to highlight the skills and values you communicated to us."

"Your long tenure at Sarah Lawrence College," Jenny said, "and your constant queries concerning how we were doing at school conveyed the value you placed on taking education seriously."

I talked about how his enthusiastic and skilled teaching showed itself in visits to his lab, where he taught us about the scientific method; through his explanations of how to calculate batting averages and the probability of a "seven" showing up when rolling a pair of dice; his ability to convey a concept through a well-told story; how he listened to a half-formed idea and suggested ways to improve it; and his willingness to disagree without being disagreeable.

"And he loved animals," Jenny said. "Our dogs were not so much pets but means to study how animals thought and learned. Hide a toy; see how long it takes to find it. Hide two toys; which one will it retrieve? What and how many words can it really understand? These experiments had caused our first dog, Suzie, to roll over with great fanfare when she decided it was time for supper and to bark ferociously whenever she heard the word 'squirrel.'"

I spoke of his loyalty to us, Sarah Lawrence College, and the United States, and Jenny talked about how we could always count on him to follow through on promises. We spoke about how we enjoyed conversations with him during long walks; the amusing letters he wrote while we were at camp; and his passion for fried foods, black coffee, pasta, jelly doughnuts, fresh fruit, and especially potatoes. "In conclusion," we said together, "we admire your commitment to do the right thing well, usually with a wry wit. And we love you very much."

We invited others to talk about their memories of Dad. The Sarah Lawrence representatives spoke of how respected he was among students and staff and how he had strengthened their premed program. Neighbors and friends talked about his devotion to Pat. "I wish I could have known Rolf better," Lisa said, "but I'll always remember a conversation we had about science six months ago."

As we thanked the guests for coming, I noticed how we all were more at peace than those of us who attended my stepmother Pat's assembly-line funeral at that Trenton Catholic church. *Yes, ceremonies can be powerful catalysts toward healing and renewal,* I thought, *but this time we allowed people to speak about their memories of Dad in a safe place.* And that had made all the difference.

Two days later, Lisa and I made passionate love in the bed that Dad and Pat had slept in together for more than forty years. "They're smiling down at us," she said as we cleaned up our mess.

⁓

THE PACE OF MY SECOND visit to Columbia in early August wasn't as hectic as my July visit in part because of the energy-sapping heat. Once again,

I tried to adjust to the family's grooves as Jules and their poodle, Luke, bickered about who was top dog. We visited the local pool in the afternoon and walked around the neighborhood in the late evening. I read to the boys and tried to teach Ana to sing. We played cards and threw pillows at each other. I treated the family to pizza and frozen custard and took part in the early stages of Ana's all-night sixteenth birthday party. We explored a house that Lisa and I were thinking of buying, but couldn't negotiate a fair price with the seller. I tried to support her as she continued her divorce battle.

"What's next?" we asked ourselves during constant phone calls after Jules and I returned to my DC apartment. When should I move? Should we wait for the divorce to become final? Should I live with the family or first find a place to rent? What kind of job did I want? How could we best work with each other to support her kids? Could I jump from my urban bachelor lifestyle to "family man?" Were we doing the right thing? The questions went on forever without easy answers. But we spoke with counselors, friends, and lawyers until I told the landlord on the last Friday in August that Jules and I would be moving out at the end of September.

Details followed. Lisa assisted me in completing the University of Missouri's online application form so I could start applying for jobs with the largest employer in Columbia. We talked about the pros and cons of the houses that we might buy. I visited Dad and Pat's Manhattan apartment for the last time to assist Pamela in preparing for her move to northern Minnesota, where she and Happy would be living with a cousin and his family. Lisa visited me in DC one last time to help me pack and to say good-bye. And there were many ways to say good-bye: enjoying meals with friends I had made while at work; thanking those who served me at Popeyes, the China Café, Chipotle, and Manhattan Market; exchanging gifts with the person who assisted me with mail; and hanging out at the boys'-night-out get-togethers that I had helped organize four years earlier.

Linda Walters drove Jules and me to her house after movers had picked up my belongings that wouldn't fit in the two large suitcases I would be taking with me, and then drove us to Reagan National Airport the following morning.

"Thanks for everything," I said with a lump in my throat as we walked to the ticket counter.

"Don't worry; you'll do fine." We hugged as an airline employee arrived to assist me to the gate.

CHAPTER SEVENTEEN:
THREE CEREMONIES

SEPTEMBER 2006–SEPTEMBER 2007

My first forty-eight hours in Columbia were hectic. After unpacking and assisting with getting the boys ready for school, Lisa and I toured a 4,300-square-foot house and signed the papers that would make it ours. As we were waiting for the real estate agent to drive us home, she asked me what I thought of the house. I told her I loved that it was located a block away from a bus stop and near several stores and restaurants.

"But what do you think of the house?" she repeated.

"Right now, it's a huge echo-y space."

"So you don't like it."

"I don't know what to think. It's so much bigger than my DC apartment." Lisa was silent, so I reached for her hand. "I know you have big plans for this house," I told her, "and I'm confident that you'll make the space a great place for us to live."

The next day at 8:30 a.m., Lisa and Ana took me to my first home football game of the University of Missouri Tigers. "This is insane," I shouted as we walked through the smells of burnt brats and stale beer, the thuds of caught footballs, and the cacophony of raucous voices competing with blaring music, "and kick-off is still two hours away."

"Different from Ivy League football?" Lisa shouted as we approached the tent where we would be adding to the din. Soon I was munching on brats, potato salad, cheese, chips, and dips and drinking beer before noon, something I hadn't done since college. I listened as people argued about the qualities of players and coaches and gossiped about who was screwing whom. I learned that Big Twelve football fans thought of Manhattan as the home of Kansas State instead of an island on the East River and that they were suspicious of those who attended elite universities and lived in big cities. During the pregame hype in the stadium, I discovered that the best-known fight songs of Missouri and Cornell shared the same melody. During the game, I began learning the rituals connected with first downs, third downs, and touchdowns, and to loathe the Survivor song "Eye of the Tiger," which the band seemed to play every fifteen minutes. The Tigers won easily, and I savored the celebration as we walked through the post-game party back to our car.

During the next two months, Lisa and I settled into a more predictable life. We tried to persuade the night-owl boys that they wanted to go to school at eight in the morning. I rode behind Lisa on her Yamaha scooter to buy supplies, grab a meal at one of the local restaurants, or fight with contractors who were remodeling our new house. We walked around the neighborhood with Jules in harness and with Lisa and Luke observing from behind. We assisted the boys with homework and supported Ana as she dealt with high school life. We tried to keep order during rowdy dinners and to persuade the boys that they wanted to go to bed at ten p.m. I tried to support Lisa as she continued her divorce battle, and interviewed for several vacant positions at the University of Missouri. All of the hiring managers failed my disability test, and none hired me.

We moved into our new house during the late afternoon of a balmy late November day. The following evening, Lisa and I stood in our new dining room holding hands and watching the first Columbia blizzard in twenty years. The boys burst into our room at 6:30 the following morning to announce that school was canceled and that twenty inches of snow was covering the ground.

We spent the next week settling in. Lisa and Ana unpacked boxes and cooked soups and stews to combat the Arctic conditions. The boys joined neighborhood kids to sled, build forts, and throw snowballs in below-zero weather conditions, occasionally banging into the house looking for hot chocolate, dry clothes, and hugs. I assisted when I could but spent most of my time learning the layout of the house. Jules dashed around our fenced-in backyard while Luke sailed across the six-foot fence to patrol his new surroundings, often appearing at our back door covered with snow at two in the morning.

Ten days later, the balmy conditions and our more predictable life had returned, but Christmas was coming. It would be my first celebration with kids since college. I placed several ornaments on our large Christmas tree in the living room while telling the kids about how I had strung cranberries as part of our Christmas preparations. I formed cookie dough into various shapes as part of Lisa's cookie-baking and fudge-making spree as Christmas music filled the kitchen. I watched some of the corny Christmas movies that I had slept through while growing up. As Lisa prepared her Christmas cards, I created new melodies for the texts of three familiar carols, recorded the arrangements in the downstairs cellar, and burnt them onto CDS, which were mailed with her Christmas cards. Lisa and I shared Christmas memories to the sounds of carols playing softly: how her family celebrated on Christmas Day while mine celebrated on Christmas Eve; how Mom had brailled many of the Christmas tags so I could distribute presents; the games, books, drum kit components, and other presents I had received and the gifts I had made for others; how music-making at the local Catholic and Lutheran churches had added a spiritual dimension to our celebrations; and how we had splashed about in my grandmother's pool in Florida as operatic Christmas music wafted from her living room.

At seven o'clock on Christmas morning, Lisa and I groggily joined the kids for the gleeful unwrapping of presents, and twenty minutes later, all of the books, gift certificates, electronic games, theater tickets, clothes, cosmetics, and candy were piled on chairs and tables with the wrapping paper strewn over the living room floor. Luke and Jules had received and ignored their presents. I was veging on one of our new couches, enjoying the commotion winding down around me until Joseph told me that my present was being moved to the cellar. I followed the rest of the family downstairs and found everybody admiring the components of a new drum kit.

Lisa put her arms around me. "Merry Christmas," she cooed in my ear.

After thanking everyone and assisting the boys in putting the kit together, I tried to talk to Lisa and Ana in the kitchen as the kids took turns christening the new toy. I got my chance several hours later.

~

DURING THE NEXT THREE MONTHS, I took part in more unsuccessful job interviews at the University of Missouri. While disappointed that my job search had yet to bear fruit, I wasn't particularly surprised because it had always been hard to find a job. I had spent several hours each week scouring newspapers and other sources for open positions in human resources, project management, social services, and management that matched my skills, first with the help of sighted friends and later using the Internet. I had crafted and sent numerous cover letters and résumés first by mail and then by e-mail. While incredibly frustrating at times, I had always found a job within six months, so I continued doing what had worked for me in the past.

And I kept busy. I tried to be a good role model for the kids. I took an advanced nonfiction writing course, climbing icy snow mounds with Jules in order to get to class. I visited the dentist for the first time in twenty-eight years. And I joined the choir of the Missouri United Methodist Church (MUMC for short), the largest church in Columbia.

In early February, Lisa's divorce became official, and their cat, Tiger, disappeared. Lisa and Ana searched for him for nearly a month before finding him sleeping in the sun on a neighbor's driveway. He sulked in our garage for two days, refusing to eat his favorite foods, and bolted back to the neighbor as soon as someone opened the garage door. Several days later, his new caretakers apologetically informed us that "Deuteronomy" had decided to move in with them. Like Lisa, Tiger had ended an unhealthy relationship.

My mom, my sister, Jenny, her daughter, Jessy, and Aunt Connie arrived two days before my fiftieth birthday. As Lisa guided them through the house, they oohed and ahhed at the hardwood floors, the kitchen that she had transformed into an airy welcoming place with plenty of counter space, the elegant dining room, and the downstairs bedrooms. Louis showed off his Lego collection. Joseph showed off his model airplanes and his pet python Monty, who had escaped the previous evening. We had frantically searched throughout the house until Ana found it wrapped around the wires connecting the TV with the VCR. "A good thing," Lisa told my family, "because we didn't want you to find him sleeping in your bed."

To begin the formal birthday celebration, we put on "fifty is nifty" T-shirts that Mom had brought with her and made a racket on recorders, kazoos, and drums in honor of the loud noises I had made growing up. After dinner and some silly songs composed in my honor, I announced it was time to move to the living room.

"Wait a minute," the adults protested. "It's time for cake."

"Sorry," I said as the kids and I headed there.

Grumbling good-naturedly, they followed us, settling into couches and chairs. I put a CD containing a track I had prepared for the occasion into a CD player, placed a small box on top of the piano, and faced my audience.

"I'm dedicating this song from my favorite composer, Stephen Sondheim, from my favorite Broadway show, *Sweeny Todd,* to my favorite woman," I said, trying not to choke up.

I sang about how demons will charm for a while but that "nothing's gonna harm you, not while I'm around." After the last chords died away, I became aware of the sounds of women sobbing. This startled me because no one but Lisa had ever cried after I had sung to them. And there hadn't been much crying in our house. But I forged ahead, opening the small box and taking out a ring that Lisa and I had bought together on Valentine's Day. She flung her arms around me; I asked her to marry me.

She sobbed harder.

"Will you marry me?" I repeated.

"I think you know the answer," Mom sobbed from across the room. "Lisa, will you—"

"Yes, yes," she wailed, taking the ring from my hand and putting it on her finger.

We all recovered over ice cream and cake.

Joyous peals of bird songs announced the arrival of spring. I started working Jules around the neighborhood using routes that a Guiding Eyes instructor had assisted us in learning the previous fall. He had also noticed the close bond between Lisa and her standard poodle, and had encouraged her to find a way to make him feel more "useful." So she had experimented working him in harness. "He loved it," Lisa said breathlessly. "His head and tail were in the air as he pranced. 'Look at me,' he seemed to say, 'I'm a poodle doing something important.'"

We bought Luke a cheap harness so that I could work him, as his pull was too strong for Lisa. He reminded me of Heidi the Weimaraner: strong pull, exuberant pace, and straight street crossings. But after several blocks, he started stopping short to lift his leg on bushes and fire hydrants, dragging me off the sidewalk to scent-sniff or bolt after something, barking at a creature crossing our path, or running me into trees or telephone poles.

"Not quite ready for prime time," I said, rubbing a bruise on my thigh, "but he could have been a great guide dog ... for the right person."

"And he's learned all this just by watching Jules."

I told Lisa that he wasn't much different from my other dogs. Gifford had stopped short to lift his leg on objects, and Heidi would snatch paper cups, napkins, cigarette butts, and candy wrappers from sidewalks as we prowled the Manhattan streets. "No!" I would shout, sticking my hand in her mouth to remove whatever treasure she had found.

"I would also feel her body bend low to the ground as she stalked pigeons," I continued as Lisa pleaded with Jules to walk by her side instead of three feet behind her.

"In harness? But didn't you correct her?"

"I tried, but it was pointless. She didn't slow down very much and never ran me into anything. But it was a bit much when she tried to climb the wall of a building in hot pursuit. 'You get that damn bird!' a pedestrian had shouted from across the street as I was working her home from Grand Central Station."

I continued interviewing for jobs both at the university and other organizations in the area. Several hiring managers passed my "disability test" ... but chose to hire someone else. Frustrated, I began wondering if any employer in Columbia, Missouri, would ever hire me. I had sent countless applications, taken part in numerous interviews, and networked with professionals. I understood that I was a far-from-perfect fifty-year-old man with roots in big cities competing with locals for scarce jobs in a lousy economy, but for the first time, I felt forced to grapple with how my blindness factored into this mix. I sensed that most hiring managers most of the time wanted to do the right thing, but they seemed less exposed to persons with visible disabilities serving in professional roles than those whom I worked with on the East Coast. But I now had someone who unquestionably was in my corner, and that gave me the courage to carry on the search.

In late May, Lisa and I began planning for our wedding. We decided to schedule it on a September Saturday when the Missouri Tigers football team wouldn't be playing at home; that the ceremony and reception would take place in our backyard; that my favorite cousin, Hale, would be best man and that her daughter, Ana, would be maid of honor; that my DC friend Gordon would provide the reception music—

"What's wrong?" Lisa asked when I was quiet for too long.

"Nothing. I've just composed the first eight measures of our wedding processional."

~

"WHAT DO YOU MEAN YOU didn't give us Joseph's tux?" I shouted over the phone an hour before the scheduled start of our wedding. I slammed the cordless phone into its cradle as the noise of people running around the house looking for clothes and taking care of last-minute details seeped through the closed door of the master bedroom.

Lisa came out of the bathroom. "What's wrong? And you shouldn't be here." She steered me out of the room. "Figure it out," she snapped through the closed door.

"I'll take care of it," promised a neighbor I barely knew. She hurried out of the house as Jules and I trudged downstairs to one of the bedrooms where some of the men were changing into wedding clothes.

"Why tuxes?" groused Mitch, one half of the couple who had introduced me to Lisa and a groomsman. We were not looking forward to sweltering in early evening steam-bath conditions.

"It won't be that bad," called another groomsman from the opposite corner. Dave was totally blind and had been a leader of a nationwide group of students I had organized fifteen years earlier as part of my efforts to improve employment opportunities for college students with disabilities. We had remained friends as he had morphed from college dorm manager to cross-country skier to seller of technology to agencies serving blind people.

"But don't you live in Arkansas?" Mitch challenged as peals of laughter from the bridal party filtered down from the master bedroom.

Upstairs, I sat on a living room couch with Jules under my feet, trying to read a magazine. But I couldn't concentrate. Our wedding preparations had been sandwiched around boys' baseball, the Fourth of July festivities, and family trips to Minneapolis to attend the ACB convention, to Cape Cod to visit Mom and Jenny, and to Lisa's timeshare near Branson. Lisa and I had spent hours discussing wedding plans. We had stayed up all night stuffing envelopes with invitations. We had prepared programs in regular print, large print, and braille. We had negotiated with caterers and met with a MUMC minister to guide us through the ceremony. We had decided to spend our honeymoon in Jamaica at a recently opened Sandals forty-five minutes east of Negril. Lisa had rented tables, chairs, and linens. She had found a photographer and worked with a florist, ignoring my suggestion that vases of Venus Flytraps be placed on each table to feast on bugs that would otherwise annoy those at the reception. I had composed and recorded the wedding music while assisting Gordon and his wife, Janiece, in handling the rest of the entertainment.

But I began wondering if the wedding would take place as people scurried down our thirteen hardwood stairs through the downstairs living room to the backyard to address last-minute details. Did the caterers need guidance? Were all the decorations in place—

"This tux is stupid," Joseph complained. "It's too hot, and ..." His voice faded away as Rich, an executive who had mentored me at that London-based corporation and my third groomsman, hustled him downstairs.

"Marisha, would you take those champagne glasses downstairs?" Lisa asked from the master bedroom. "And the programs—"

"Sorry to bother you, but it's time for the wedding pictures," the photographer mumbled in my ear.

"Outside. And where's the guest—"

A shriek, shattering glass, a body crashing down the stairs. Stunned silence.

And this wasn't the first time a member of the wedding party had fallen down a flight of stairs. During the wedding shower two days earlier, a friend of Lisa's who could "see just enough to be dangerous" had twisted her knee as she fell down several stairs at the Country Club of Missouri. Ana had sat with her in the emergency room as Lisa had dashed about town doing last-minute errands, and I had found a wheelchair for her friend to use.

"Are you all right?" several people shouted. Marisha didn't move.

"What's wrong?" Lisa called.

People carefully approached Marisha to assess the damage and to clean up the shattered glass.

"What's wrong?" Lisa repeated.

"Everything's fine," I called, now worried that the wedding would have to be rescheduled. Marisha still hadn't made a sound.

"What's wrong?" Lisa demanded, hurrying to the stairs. "My God! Are you okay?" Marisha groaned. "Don't move!"

"I think she's fine," Rich said, "but it wouldn't hurt if a doctor checked her out."

"She appears to be fine," a neighborhood doctor confirmed several minutes later, "but she should take it easy for the rest of the day."

"I think I'm going to faint," Lisa wailed several minutes later as the wedding party milled about in the downstairs living room, waiting for Gordon and Janiece to start playing the opening song.

"I can't believe this is happening," Mom said as she brushed something off of my shirt over the calming noises coming from Lisa's direction.

We all relaxed when we heard the opening chords of "Seasons of Love" from the Broadway musical *Rent* floating through the closed door, knowing that the wedding would indeed take place and that everything would be fine. As Gordon and Janiece sang about how relationships are built minute by minute and the importance of treasuring moments together, we organized ourselves for the trip outside. Then came the percussion riff that began the processional I had written for this moment, and my favorite cousin, Hale, escorted Jules and me to a towering oak tree where the ceremony would take place.

"You're going to be fine," said the pastor who would be leading the ceremony as Jules lay down with a grunt and started crunching a stick.

"I hope so," I said, as people started moving into position around me: the three groomsmen and my best man, Hale; the three bridesmaids and Ana serving as maid of honor; my sister's daughter, Jessy, as flower girl; and Lisa's youngest son, Louis, and a girl from the neighborhood as ring-bearers.

"Here comes Lisa. She looks beautiful," the pastor said as she approached with her oldest son, Joseph, and Luke the poodle.

"I hope they make it down here before the music ends," I grumbled. They did ... barely.

The ceremony flew by. After welcoming remarks and a reading about love from First Corinthians, I sang an Al Jareau song to Lisa about "the knight in shining armor faithful and true" and that "after all, I will be the one to hold you in my arms," accompanied by a track that Gordon had created. The pastor assisted Lisa and me in exchanging vows, rings, and a kiss, and then led Lisa, her kids, and me to commit to doing our best to make this new family work. Gordon and Janiece sang "Love Changes Everything" from Andrew Lloyd Webber's musical, *Aspects of Love*, as each of us put a flower into a vase to symbolize this commitment. After closing remarks from the pastor, Lisa and I hurried to accept congratulations from well-wishers as the wedding recessional I had written competed with applause and preparations for the reception.

"Congratulations!" squealed Donna, one of the bridesmaids and the other half of the couple who had introduced us. As Lisa and Donna hugged, Mitch made halfhearted congratulatory noises and asked if he could get rid of his tux.

"Fine with me. I only wish I could," I grumbled over the disapproving clucks of the women. He kept his tux on.

As Gordon started playing music for the reception, the congratulations continued. The other groomsmen and bridesmaids. Mom, Jenny, and Jessy, who talked with Lisa about the quick glances and brief headshakes between them that had prevented them from crying during the Al Jareau song. Aunt Connie from France who had told us that she couldn't come but had shown up anyway. Aunt Sibyl with her two adult children and their spouses. Pamela, Dad and Pat's live-in housekeeper, and Jim, their longtime Trenton friend. Becky of Guiding Eyes who hugged me while her guide dog and Jules strained to greet each other. Betina, a University of Missouri English professor who had started me on my journey as an author. Staff from It's a Grind, a coffee shop where Luke had barked at customers as Lisa drank vanilla lattés, and where Jules had slept as I wrote and sipped passion fruit iced teas. Dick, a counselor who had supported us as we worked through our relationship kinks. Members of Lisa's family. Ana's high school friends who described how they had turned in their seats at the beginning of "Seasons of Love" expecting a recording but seeing live performers. Lisa's friends from high school and college, members of the MUMC choir, and others who I barely knew. All of the congratulatory showers felt nice, but a shower of breezy rain to break the tropical spell would have been nicer; it was too damned steamy for a tux.

After the reception line, Lisa and I returned to the quiet, cool house, where I left Jules to chill and ditched my tux jacket. We reentered the steamy noise, wandering from table to table, soaking in the festive atmosphere and becoming drenched in congratulatory compliments until something poked my leg.

"What are you doing here, Luke?" I asked, brushing his head as he pranced by. "How did you get out?"

Lisa sighed. "Not much we can do about it," she said as we prepared to kick off the dancing.

We continued to roam, this time sitting at random tables. With a beer in my hand and my butt in a chair, I could relax enough to absorb some of the compliments. The local prosecuting attorney proclaimed that he had bawled during the Al Jareau song after not crying for twenty-five years. Ana's friends marveled that Gordon sang and played keyboards, trumpet, and saxophone, and that he could play keyboards with one hand while using his other hand to play one of his horns—

"Luke just ate Gordon's plate of food while he was singing," Aunt Sibyl's son reported.

People loved our backyard, the flowers, the furniture, the tent—

"Luke is peeing on all the rented plants," Lisa told me in a voice of amused horror.

My wedding processional had grabbed the attention of MUMC's senior minister. People raved about the food—

"That horrible black dog just stole a cracker from a child's hand," Mom told us.

Then it was cake-cutting time. "Don't worry," Gordon had said during one of our wedding-planning conversations. "Just follow what I'm singing, and everyone—blind and sighted—will know what's happening." So we made our way to the proper place after sending someone to alert him that we were getting ready. We were stopped by Olie, the Norwegian-born husband of Aunt Sibyl's daughter, who started rhapsodizing about the wedding.

"Folks," Gordon announced over the PA system. "They're getting ready to cut the cake."

"Wait!" we yelled.

"… so lovely; the yard, the trees, the flowers, the tent—"

"Thanks, Olie," we said, as Gordon started singing about how the bride was picking up the knife.

"… and the ceremony was so beautiful—"

"Thanks, Olie," we said, "but we're getting ready to cut the cake."

"The bride cuts the cake," Gordon sang.

"Wait!" several people yelled.

"... and the food, the people! Everything's so wonderful—"

"The bride feeds the groom," Gordon sang.

"Olie, *move!*" we yelled.

"Oh," he said as we hurried past him to the table, arriving just in time to hear Gordon singing about the groom feeding the bride.

We made Gordon repeat the song, and following his directions, Lisa cut the three-tiered cake decorated to match the autumn leaves on our invitations. We fed each other a mixture of white cake, chocolate cake, and raspberry filling. It was delicious.

I was tired of the steamy noise and being the center of attention. I wanted to ditch my tux and chill with Jules in the cool, quiet house, but I had to endure the toasts and the endless posing for pictures and the throwing of the bouquet and more wedding chatter until I heard Rich say that he was heading for the house to change out of his tux. I leapt to my feet. "Can I go with you?" I shouted.

"Sure," he said. I latched onto his elbow.

"Peter, no," Lisa pleaded, but I was gone.

After the reception ended thirty minutes later, several close friends and family joined Lisa and me in the downstairs cellar, eventually forming an impromptu drum circle that I led from my new drum kit as Ana slept in her room across the hall. Two hours later, weird leaf-like objects stuck to my back as I crawled into bed while Lisa was downstairs talking with the boys.

Her wails startled me awake some time later. I leapt out of bed and hugged her. "Life's so short," she said through her tears. "We can't afford to let things slide by."

Baffled, I let my social-work side make random, comforting noises. "After all," I sang, "I will be the one to hold you in my arms," we sang together.

We compared notes as we sat together in our jet tub. The bridal party had bonded over massages, lunch, and hairstyling while the men had bonded over beers, burgers, buffalo wings, potato skins, portabella fries, and other bar food. We marveled at how well the wedding had gone despite the last-minute Dunbar Factors. "And did you hear what the photographer said?" Lisa asked as the bath water gurgled down the drain.

"No."

"He said that he's shot many weddings over the years and can tell if a marriage will work or not ... and that we will make it."

"And what are these things?" I asked, waving another leaf-like object in her direction.

"They're rose petals. Aren't they romantic?"

And though we were tired, we couldn't fall asleep until we learned that the Tigers had beaten some Mississippi school on the road; after all, it was Big Twelve football season.

The next morning, many of us slogged through another steamy day to attend the eleven o'clock church service at MUMC, where I would be singing in the choir and Lisa would be baptized. Several weeks earlier, she had surprised me with her decision to commit to making the Christian journey because of her prior complaints about the conniving adulterous know-it-alls that she had met who bragged about their church attendance. I had told her that I had been baptized when I was seventeen in a private ceremony because I was afraid of the outpouring of praise I might receive; how Saturday-night partying and my circle of friends had discouraged me from attending services in college; how my feeble efforts to return to church had been thwarted when ushers at one church wouldn't let me enter with my guide dog and ushers at another wanted me to sit in a balcony instead of among the congregation; and my irritation with people who preached at me on the street about how I was blind because I didn't have enough faith. I had rarely attended church services during my urban bachelor lifestyle days because I treasured the chance to relax on Sundays after a hard week's work.

"But several Christian radio preachers caught my attention," I told Lisa, "when they described how God influenced events through far-from-perfect kings, prophets, and disciples." I talked about how while working toward my social work degree, I had been surprised by the agreements between "secular" and "Christian" counselors despite the contempt that both groups expressed toward each other. Somehow, the salvation message had seeped into my soul despite my irritation with preachers who railed against sexual sins at the expense of other misdeeds; how they demonized those who disagreed with them; and how the sins of women and people without money seemed more harmful than those of men and people with money.

Lisa had started attending services after I had joined the choir, and we had both come to appreciate the church's welcoming spirit and creative music ministry. As I witnessed her baptism and joined her to become members, I was surprised by the waves of thanks and joyous peace that flooded my soul.

The wedding wind-down continued. After brunch at a local restaurant, we lounged around our house saying our thanks and good-byes as people returned to their homes in New York, New Jersey, DC, Virginia, Missouri, Massachusetts, Minnesota, California, Colorado, Florida, Kentucky, Arkansas, Oregon, and Roscoff, France. We returned the rented tuxes and sound equipment, ate wedding leftovers, and admired the pile of wedding gifts on our dining room table. Then came the frantic packing for our ten-day Jamaican honeymoon and last-minute good-byes and instructions to Ana, who would be looking after her brothers and the dogs. We wheeled our luggage through the beginnings of a breezy rain shower into the van that would take us to the St. Louis airport.

"My wuh-wuh-wife and I need help," I explained to an airport official while trying to resolve a last-minute hassle.

"What do you mean, wuh-wuh-wife?" Lisa harrumphed as we waited to board the plane.

Luke standing in front of house

Taken on March 5, 2007 during Peter's 50th birthday celebration

Peter, Lisa, and family at University of Missouri Tigers home football game

Linda Walters and Gifford

EPILOGUE:
FAMILY MAN

FEBRUARY, 2012

Ana is a junior at the University of Missouri, exploring her interests in East Asian studies, cultural anthropology, and fine art. Joseph is a high school freshman playing defensive lineman for the football team. Louis is an eighth grader interested in computer programming. Lisa has finished her PhD coursework and is experimenting with pig aortas to try to develop a decellularized scaffold for use as vascular grafts in people.

Jules is eight years old and in good health. While he works less because of the distances between places and Columbia's reliance on cars instead of public transportation, we still walk at least a mile a day around the neighborhood. He still greets me by squeezing headfirst between my legs, and occasionally steals bread and everything bagels.

Shortly after the wedding, the family started calling Jules a "Dalmatian in reverse" and a "mutant Labrador" because of the mysterious spots that had begun appearing on his face and haunches soon after I moved to Columbia. He wagged his tail and smiled as Guiding Eyes staff crowded around him during a reception at an ACB convention in Louisville,

Kentucky, to take pictures on their cell phones that were e-mailed to their breeding expert. He wags his tail and smiles as strangers tell him that the spots make him look more distinguished.

During the past year, Jules's pace has slowed, and his enthusiasm for the work has been waning. A Guiding Eyes instructor has encouraged me to retire him within a year. When the time comes, he will enjoy a quieter life with Pat and Linda Walters in northern Virginia while I begin the bonding process with a new dog.

The Guiding Eyes facilities have undergone a transformation since Jules and I began working together. Students now stay in single rooms where they can bond with their new dogs in peace. The campus also contains a revolving door and elevator on which dogs and students receive training, as well as a game/music room, fitness center, and technology lab.

Training processes and methods have also evolved. "We focus more on building that relationship between handler and dog," Graham told me, "and we want to provide more tools for the handler to encourage the dog when it is performing well."

Two new poodles have joined our family: Heidi, a nine-month-old standard named in honor of my first guide dog; and Hunter, a playful eight-month-old male who Lisa says looks like a skunk. Every morning, dogs growl, bark, leap, and cavort about my feet. "Peter?" Lisa shouts over the din.

"Coming," I call, hurrying upstairs with dogs thundering behind.

"Perhaps Heidi or Hunter might be your next guide dog?" Lisa asks with a smile in her voice.

I still haven't found a job, but I'm still working: serving as member of a council of Guiding Eyes graduates that assists the school in developing programs and marketing their services. Waking the boys up on school days. Supporting organizations as they develop strategic plans and address diversity-related conflicts. Loading and unloading the dishwasher. Writing an article about the Reverse Mentoring Program that was posted on the Best Practices Institute's website. Taking out the trash. Serving on the editorial board of *Syndicated Columnists Weekly*, a well-respected magazine for blind people. Doing laundry. Organizing two job fairs in conjunction with ACB conventions. Herding poodles. Serving as president of Friends-in-Art of ACB. Keeping the family appointment calendar. Serving as MUMC's composer-in-residence. Learning to be a better husband …